# LOVE NEVER DIES

Love Never Dies is dedicated to my Graham.

As Rumi said: "Lovers don't finally meet somewhere. They're in each other all along."

Profits from this book will be donated to pancreatic cancer research

# THE ROBIN

I found this definition on Google and it sums up perfectly why the beautiful bird of winter HAD to be my book cover

"The robin has so much to teach you in life, is a sacred bird, that offers protection and spiritual enlightenment.

In short, the spiritual meaning of a robin includes: transformation, growth, renewal, passion, change, and power.

The robin is all about perseverance and trying to 'keep on keeping on'.

The robin is a sign that you should listen to the song of your heart".

# TESTIMONIALS

"Angela's experience of loss is not the same as mine and mine will not be the same as yours but   by putting her feelings into words she makes a key connection with every one of us who has had to let go of someone they did love and will always love dearly. The upside , if there is one, is that Angela is absolutely right....love never dies. My parents might not be 'here' but they are always with me."
Kaye Adams, Broadcaster

"Love Never Dies describes beautifully what we all feel before, during and after the loss of a loved one. It puts into words what we feel and validates our feelings making us feel less alone and more connected to others. It takes the fear from the dying process and makes it more normal, which it is, as part of the circle of life."
I LOVED it!
Dr Mary Frame,
Retired GP and retired Specialty Doctor at Marie Curie Hospice.

"Love Never Dies speaks to everyone who has experienced the loss of a loved one – and that is just about everyone. Angela brings the message of the power of love in a comforting and healing voice. Truly, a lovely book."
Caroline Myss, Author of Anatomy of the Spirit and Defy Gravity

# CHAPTER 1: THE BEGINNINGS

BEE ALIVE

I found a dying bee on the kitchen window ledge very early this morning. It was exhausted. It looked like I felt - done in.

Sleep came easy last night but didn't last long. The 4am tribunal arrived bang on time.

Many of you have shared your stories of losing loved ones, and I'm truly grateful. Sometimes the discussions arise on the pros and cons of a sudden death - quick but shocking, and no time to say things that mattered; or a forewarned end - drip-fed grieving, watching the loved one suffer, but time to say what mattered.

Either way, it's shite. Really shite. There is no way to escape the dark night of the soul.

With the morning mist early this morning, came the gremlins. The love and light had dimmed, and what came into focus were the shitty times. All of them, in a oner.

The times my father wasn't there, the times he'd hurt me, the arguments, the let-downs, his flaws and defects, his angry moments with me, times I'd felt rejected, excluded, abandoned, times of estrangement in the past.

All my indignant rage and fury surfaced into a massive wave of "How dare he have treated me like that, how very DARE HE?".

Meanwhile, a part of me was observing all of this tumultuous outrage, and feeling horrified at myself for even going near this stuff just now, while he lives and breathes.

Regardless, I dived in to the anger - I felt it all with every part of me. "I hate you! I hate you Dad!"

It was maybe 15 mins, maybe an hour later... all of the ways I had let HIM down, broken his heart, disappointed him, abandoned, rejected, verbally attacked him, appeared on the horizon, and rolled towards me like a Tsunami.

I nearly drowned under its force.

When I was five, on a family holiday in Millport at Crocodile Rock, I drowned. Out cold. I'd wandered in after an uncle and fell off the shelving sands. My father, with his shirt off and trousers rolled up, was lighting his pipe on the beach.

He flew in, dived in, found me, and resuscitated me. He brought me back to life.

As I lay in bed, curtains open, this morning I cried a prayer of forgiveness to my Dad through the ether, and asked him to forgive me.

The swifts started up their dawn performance, always in pairs. Jonathan Livingston Seagull did a short solo ballet, and the black-birds accompanied as a choir.

I don't know how they learned the theme from Frozen, MY God, she moves in mysterious ways, but sing it they did.

"Let it go, let it goooooo"

I gave the dying bee sugar water, and carried it outside on to some clover. Just before I wrote this a bee (who knows?) flew back in, then out of the kitchen door.

REASONS TO BE CHEERFUL

Dougie sent me the most beautiful of songs, that sustained him through the hard times of his losses. Thank you.

A thoughtful client brought Ferrero Rocher, who had heard through the grapevine.

My next book is called Feel the Fat And Eat Them Anyway.

Thank you. Laura gave me a soul-soothing facial. Thank you.

Robert gave me a restorative hug. Thank you.

Irene checked on my vitamins and supplements supplies, and shared life-affirming laughter at daft stories about ma Da. Thank you.

Lord G sorted out a wee night away at Pitlochry on Saturday for my dad's birthday present to me to see Carousel. David and Tara have agreed to accompany us. Dad, Mags and us have gone for last few years, and he should've been there. Thank you.

Marion called to check on me, Maureen was hovering around with her support and beautiful words of support. Shirley appeared like an angel out of the blue and surrounded me with her peace and empathy.

She lost her parents and sister in recent years. Thank you ladies.

Ashley, my niece told me how much she wants to be there for me. And Sir Ian the cat cuddled in for a Cat Hug. Thank you, and meow. How lucky am I?

PRE-EMPTIVE GRIEF

This vicious type of grief affects different people in different ways. Nothing has actually "happened" yet, but we know it will.

So we try to take control of the situation; staying busy, trying to prepare in advance, trying to process, trying to act "normal". And all the time, there is a train on the horizon coming down the track towards us - we can't tell its speed from where we are but we know it's coming.

The support that friends, and often strangers, offer at this time is like an anchor, securing me in stormy and relentless seas.

The calm that settles from another's shared story of a similar or previous journey steadies my heart. Beautiful gestures, like our Garden Fairy Helper who arranged a vase of flowers from the garden in a vase, and left them on the kitchen table. Genuine offers of practical help, like the relative who works in London offering to help in the Clinic in Glasgow if required.

Spontaneous and tentative phone calls from people not seen for years who start "I hope I'm not intruding, or being inappropriate, but.."

Then there are the deeply connected conversations that explore uncharted territory with an aunt, a friend, a colleague. Loving words, uncensored tears.

Then the freak waves hit. Dealing with the painful, thoughtless fallout of others' grief reactions to the situation. The "friend" who knows yet remains silent for weeks.

The mindless pettiness, the scapegoating, the controlling behaviour, as taking control becomes more important than taking care. It is easier to be angry at times like this for some - the territory is more familiar.

Our good friend Anger, is a powerful shipmate in the storms. Familiar and reliable! Instant release of the inner tensions. It attaches itself to trivia, details, competition and Ego....."I think....", "I want"....

Surrender is much tougher. To feel the fear, to hold the anxiety.

It's at times like this you know, no, really FEEL who has your back. Marion, my fellow therapist and practice manager has been amazing. Never off duty.

I'm thinking of writing another book - it's called Feel the Fear and Pee Yourself Anyway!

To tie yourself to the mast and let the winds howl around you and pray God you will reach safe harbour repeating the Mantra over and over, "I am powerless".

That's where I found my strength and my peace as I watched the sun rise this morning, and the first blackbirds sang from the telephone wires outside my window.

# CHAPTER 2: JULY 2016

TREE AND EASY

Oh my God. I've been busy hacking at tree roots, doing a Chainsaw Massacre and driving in a hire van like Rambo all day, then switched on my phone to find a tsunami of love and support on my FB page.

God bless each and every one of you. I'm blown away by your love. How utterly beautiful.

My post started as a "musing" on my meditation and grew and grew. To be honest the garden turmoil was a good foil for worry and angst but I'm ready for a bath and an early night now. You are all in my heart. Thank you beautiful soul sisters and brothers xxx

DIGGING DEEP

Spent a heartful day with mum, and ate a full and guilt-free afternoon tea (left half a scone.) We laughed at daft memories, cried, held hands, hugged deeply. We women dig deep. We sat in her beautiful garden with Boo the Scarecrow.. he didn't scare us. We spoke about closure and how important that is in life. My dad's very ill, and my parents divorced many years ago.

GREET PRAY LOVE

Going up to see dad today. His meds have been upped and he has doesn't eat much, sleep doesn't come easy. We text sometimes during the night, while the world sleeps, and "meet" in meditation in a beautiful place where he and I are pain-free.

I thought I'd share a chat we had, just he and I, on regrets, forgiveness and screwing up. He was anxious about his mistakes, people he'd hurt, things he'd got wrong, and how clear it was now that love is all that matters.

I disagreed. I said "You're wrong Dad! Screwing up, getting it wrong, making an arse of it, hurting others is where it's at!"

He looked perplexed. So did I, 'cos I had absolutely NO idea where I was going with this one, but my mouth kept moving anyway.

"It is absolutely crucial for our souls to grow, that we blow it regularly. If we are here to learn how to love, how to forgive, how to develop compassion (which I believe we are), how are we gonna do that sitting on a beach, drinking wine, smoking cigars and singing Kumbaya? If everyone is yer pal, and loves you to the moon and back, we'd stagnate.

No! I learn the art of forgiveness and how to love with compassion by getting down there in the mire, by getting up weary in the morning and dealing with the face in the mirror... and learning to FORGIVE MYSELF.

Then we start to learn how to FORGIVE THEM. One spoonful at a time. And as we do one, it helps do the other. And on it goes.....

If no-one ever "stands on my foot", and gives me the gift of something to forgive them for, how am I gonna get the practice in? And I need to do my fair share of giving folks something to practice with too. By God, I do. We ALL do!

If I was your guardian angel, and my job was to develop your soul in this lifetime , I'd plan a lot of useful "learning exercises and experiences" for you along the way. Big screw-ups. Big let downs. I would, however, not tire you out, and I'd intersperse it with joy, bliss, laughter, beaches, wine and cigars. And of course the occasional chorus of Kumbaya to break the monotony. So endeth the lesson."

He smiled and I smiled. We sat silent for quite some time.

# CHAPTER 3 : AUGUST 2016

THROUGH THE WALL

Came back today via dad's. He had a bad day yesterday and marginally better today. I saw a big change in the week I was away. I'm glad I came back; I had considered a couple of nights in a Hotel as petrol in my tank. But Sister Jean and I had a chat, and my intuition kicked in to return.

His plans to go up to Tighnabruaich were kicked into touch after yesterday. I'm staying overnight here tonight. I think it's gonna be a long night as I plan to send Distance Reiki for some time through the wall to where he sleeps next door. We chatted with Uncle David (Priest) about his Funeral, which he is working on himself.

It's surreal in one sense - and so intimate and realistic, raw and awake, in another. We talked about how as his external life is diminishing, and with it his focus and interest in "material /external" things; his inner life, inner landscape and spiritual life are growing and developing. And bizarrely, how much he is enjoying planning his own funeral.

They've asked me to sing a Gaelic hymn.....I said I'd be honoured. Can I do it? Heaven knows..

DAD'S ARMY

Sir Ian has decided to join me in daily meditation. He uses a mantra "Feed me, feed me". It is nice, though the purring can become a distraction.

I then went for a lovely walk with a Butterfly (Flutter-by) for company a good part of the journey. It was, in fact, the colour of butter, and danced along the hedgerow, stopping every few flowers or so.

Saw Dad yesterday - thinner still, tired sooner, but still laughing. He acted out the parts of his recent discovery of the brilliance of the original Dad's Army TV show.

He didn't "get it" when it was out originally. He gets it now, the timing, the quick wit, his favourite line is "You STUPID BOY". And he adores Captain Mainwaring.

He told us how he so wanted to join up and do his National Service, to get a uniform but had TB so ended up in Civil Service instead.

He'd love a uniform. Must find a shop that sells military hats.. it's never too late to be a Captain. My Captain.

GOT THE HAT!

Continuing on from my last post (pardon the pun ) about my dad's disappointment at not being selected for the forces to do his National Service because he was desperate to wear a uniform.. I finally sourced the HAT, which I will confer on him on Monday.

And discovered it just along from The Harvest Clinic at the Arty Party Shop.

I was mildly rattled that the ex-military uniform Shop in King St couldn't get me a British Captain's hat but could offer me a German WW2 version for £700.

Now, I love my da but I realise, it is conditional.

MEDICINAL MUSIC

I originally wanted to train as a music therapist but I wasn't good enough as a late starter for the entry requirements at London's Guildhall; I did a degree in music and psychology at Glasgow instead, got married and worked in advertising.

Five years and many burned bridges later, I trained as a Clinical Hypnotherapist but music was always my medicine. I use it a lot on my Workshops and Retreats to help people access feelings, sometimes tears and snotters; sometimes deep joy.

My father taught me the banjo when I was five - Honky Tonk Angels! I reminded him recently that the affirmation "I might have known you'd never make a wife" in the song, sung repeatedly at such a tender age, may have in no small way contributed to the subsequent failure of my first marriage.

Music has been a huge part of my dad's life - he took up Jazz Piano seriously in his late 60s. I found the song There's A Place For Us from West Side Story on his piano yesterday and I sang it. I wrote on the bottom "Yes there is, and I'll meet you there".

He wants the song played at the Crematorium, followed by HIM playing Ain't Misbehaving and Saving all my Love for You (recorded last year for his 80th).

He is really focused on preparing his last public performance.

Music heals, it opens, it is a gateway to the soul. I am certain that it will be a means of communication between us after he passes, from the Universal Heart to mine.

Play some music today, and REALLY listen to it. Let it open your heart. Have a dance around the kitchen like me.

## SLOWING THE CAROUSEL

Spent the day with my father, to give Margaret a break. He has dropped a level again in available energy and is much more frail. He sleeps a major part of the day, with just a few "good hours " in the middle. Although visitors have been marvellous and have kept his spirits up, he is now admitting it is too much for him and the visits can leave him exhausted - too many people, too long, too frequent. We will need to slow the carousel down. It is hard.

My brothers arrived and spent some time too - just the four of us for the first time since it all started. It was poignant.The bonds of love and Intimacy were palpable. I think we all drew great strength from each other. We talked about the funeral and his wishes with him. Surreal but so comforting to know what he wants, and not have a lot of confusion ahead. I am recording my Gaelic/Celtic hymn soon, so I don't need to sing on the day. We all agreed that me doing a Bette Midler Beaches performance on my knees may not be a good look.

I did, however, manage a fine performance yesterday when a wasp landed on my arm. My brothers pointed this out to me, several times: "Nope, its STILL there!", "It's up your sleeve now!"; "It's behind you". Thanks boys.

With each observation, I shook my arm VIGOROUSLY, several times, and flailed about to remove the offending demonic insect. When it finally flew away I wondered why they were both howling with laughter- hystericallly - and pointing at dad. I was confused. His shirt was soaking wet and water was dripping off his glasses and nose. He looked as if he had stood under a shower.

Then I noticed the opened bottle of water in my hand, with which I had liberally doused him. He just shook his head, and went off to change his shirt. He is well "cleansed", for the next step on his journey.

COMPASSION

I always pause, self-consciously, before writing these posts, and worry if I'm being too self-indulgent, too much. I wonder if you are thinking 'Get over it - get on with it! Spare me the details".

But then I re-read the comments, the private messages (sometimes from complete strangers who have read a Shared post) saying that they have been helped or felt supported by my thoughts. It spurs me on to risk the possibility of judgement or criticism.

So many out there are on a similar journey of grief: though their loved ones may already have passed.

Or they are dealing with the grief associated with ageing parents, disabled children, miscarriage, failing relationships, family estrangements, medical diagnoses, redundancies, and all the challenges life throws at us.

Life is suffering. We hit the stuck places; the emptiness; we walk headlong into the unknown territory.

I've done my fair share of trying out the usual anaesthetics to see if I could find some respite: denial, busyness, carbs, rose wine, compulsive cleaning, Kalms, mindless TV, even revisited my old pal from the past Ms.Silk Cut for a while to see if she could help to numb out.

Some of these very temporarily shield the feeling of my nerves being worn on the outside of my skin; but not for long and my broken heart, she waits for me in spite of my valiant efforts to hide.

"Embracing the pain, sharing what hurts the most with someone who won't invade or abandon me feels like standing on Holy Ground" - James Finley

I find the "Pearl of Great Price" - the preciousness of my fragility in my brokenness.

And I stumble upon compassion for all that's lost and broken in myself; and in others.

Richard Rohr calls it "The Naked Now". When I show up, when I am willing to experience the Good, the Bad, and the Hellish. It transforms me. I can begin to say a quiet "YES" - to ALL of it.

We can say "YES" when we don't isolate ourselves, don't pretend, and don't hide.

Today I plan to "Be Here Now". It may not last long, but with compassion for myself, I can start over again.

BE HERE NOW

Visited my Dad yesterday and we sat in the sun. The tears streamed down my face with LAUGHTER as he recalled daft stories. He has always made me laugh and now is no different. Laughter is his medicine.

I had sent him a video of Ram Dass, who he reads and loves, but he couldn't hear the words on his phone, so I paraphrased for him and he was entranced by them; comforted.

I transcribed them last night and sent them to him so he could read them again. The piece is called Be Here Now and I suggest you read it.

I wish you Love, Angela X

WEE BIRD

So, I had just sent the post "Be Here Now", and heard a rustling in the utility room. A baby bird had flown in the back door.

She was flailing about, and at one point, bounced right into the window. She fell to the floor. I lifted her out.

Sir Ian the cat thankfully asleep in the kitchen.

I placed her on the grass. Nothing. Just rolled on to her chest.

I sat on the bench with her, giving her Reiki, and prayed the Iona Healing Prayer. She sat in my open palm - blinking, sleeping, and then blinking. Nothing else, not a peep.

Graham is on retreat for two days in Elgin so nobody around to SOS.

And then, after the longest 15 minutes, she flew off into the buddleia bush.

I named her Grace.

Ps...As I write, Christy Moore is singing The First Time... "Like the trembling Heart of a captive bird".

Followed by STING If I Ever Lose My Faith In YOU.

SAYING IT BEST

There are times when we don't know what to say or do when we see others going through life's ordeals. Should we phone, write, mention it, leave them in peace, share our experiences, ask how they are, risk the tears, risk "upsetting them" risk intimacy?

A friend told me yesterday how, when her father died, she knew that someone had crossed the street to avoid her.

Everyone handles things differently, of course, and I know I have been in many situations where I've not known the RIGHT THING TO DO. And, no doubt, got it wrong for the other on many occasions.

But on discussing this with many people who have BEEN THERE before me, there seems to be a consensus that ignoring the elephant in the room is the more stressful option, by a mile.

There is something incredibly healing and comforting in the eyes of another who is willing to meet us, however tentatively and nervously, in the places that scare us both.It is true Intimacy when we risk showing up in the hurting places of life.

The isolation and feelings of alienation dissolve, and a sense of connection is found again; no matter how briefly. Loss, fear and grief are some of the loneliest paths we will ever walk.

You will, as I do, know someone out there who is in fear, who has lost (maybe even quite some time ago) or who is grieving.

Take a chance; risk it for a biscuit. Ask them how they are feeling, meet them for a coffee/lunch, send them a card, share your experience/wisdom - you may have something priceless to offer them on their journey.

Sometimes I think it's like skydiving out of a plane at night with no parachute. I have to leap first, and trust that even if I land with an almighty thud, it's just feedback for my next ascent.

There are no mistakes - none, nil, niente - when we come from our heart.

# CHAPTER 4:
# SEPTEMBER 2016

BENEFITS AND BURNS

There are some benefits to terminal illness - you get TIME, not a lot, but you get time. Downside is, you wish you'd lived like this ALL THE TIME; just making moments into memories.

Sometimes the intensity of the love and joy between family/ friends is almost too much to bear. It BURNS. Time slows down and there is a sense of tattooing on my heart the words, phrases, facial expressions and the silent communications from the gaze of my beloved Dad. I often close my eyes and just absorb his presence, so that I will recognise it more easily when he is no longer in physical form.

He loves his captain's hat and wears it to salute his guests as they leave. I will have a collection of hats I think, when he passes over the veil (currently 2 and counting).

The grandkids are amazing - so strong, brave, unselfish, loving and supportive. Wee Aiden is fast becoming the Hug Dispenser, to heal all broken hearts. He needs no Reiki training whatsoever - he is a natural.

The fruits of this challenging time are in full bloom; egos subside and souls connect and blossom.

My prayer today is Thank You.

COCOA TIME

Even as he is fully engaged in the process of dying, my father continues to inspire and educate me; every visit there is a nugget or three.

Today it was just him and I for four whole hours as M was taking a break and my beloved Lord G didn't arrive until later.

It felt like such an extravagant and abundantly boundless, timeless gift.

I held his arm as we walked the length of the street (slowly, and a little unsteadily, which is new).

I remembered the two occasions he had "walked me down the aisle" (I never do anything by halves, and you don't get rid of me easily).

I made him a smaller than before bowl of porridge for "brunch" and remembered all those winter mornings growing up, that he made the best creamy porridge in the kingdom.

He needed a rest soon after my arrival and I watched him sleep from the garden, outside the conservatory where he sat dozing.

I remembered all the bedtime stories he told me as I fell asleep with him stroking my hair and calling me his Golden Girl.

I helped him look for a lost message on his phone of a piece of music a friend had sent and noticed he had saved a message from me from back in July. It was in fact one of the posts I put on here, the Ram Dass post (BE HERE NOW).

He made me erupt with laughter with his daft stories. He calls this period in his life "cocoa time" because it's time for bed soon. It also doubles as his expression for friends who are getting on."It's cocoa time for him soon!"

He recounted stories from his life before me, and in detail how he and my mother had met; some I knew, some I didn't. I was grateful for the colouring in.

He gave me a shot of his current reading material and we had an amazing conversation about how people actually die - as in, how the spirit leaves the body.

How the Indigenous cultures learn HOW to die. I talked of my teachers Bernie Siegal/Elizabeth Khubler Ross and he shared his experience of an ever-growing knowing that there is nothing to fear about death. He experiences a familiar "presence" that he recognises from previous difficult times in his life, but which is multiplied to a huge degree now, and ever-present.

He is certain the Reiki, prayers, blessings and love directed his way and expressed in the volume of beautiful cards and letters he has been sent are helping that connection to LOVE.

I know that I can feel the wind beneath MY wings, and am sure it's pure gift from others sending me their love to sustain me.

He was fascinated when I mentioned the Native Americans' approach to dying, as he has just finished reading Black Elk, who I had read years ago.

How interesting, too, that my dad gave me my Talking Stick "Harry". It is an original Harry Lauder walking stick - long story - which I use in all my workshops/trainings. The ritual is Native Ametican.

Altogether a poignant and beautiful day, which I will treasure in my heart forever, especially when I heard him absent-mindedly sing "Kiss me, honey honey, kiss me" as I went to get him some water.

Pay attention to the little things; show up for the conversations; take their arm/hand; and don't take any of it for granted. It's all pure GIFT.

SILENT CHATS AND MIDWIVES

The Harvest Moon is a very special time for me, given my clinic is named "Harvest". It feels like a hugely significant time just now - reaping what you've sown, giving thanks, abundance, a time of transition and storing away fruits in preparation for the winter to come. A time for joy and celebration.

It's so appropriate. I know that with each day that passes, I'm moving closer to winter, when the last leaf falls and the misty, icy hush will fall.

But for now, it's time to gather in - to be grateful for the Harvest of my father's life and works. To help him gather in all the love we can as he prepares for his Journey. He is surrounded by it, thanks to so many of you who continue to send your prayers/Reiki/love/blessings.

Donna sent me a beautiful piece of writing about how we are "midwives" for our dying beloveds, and we should help to birth them over to the other side. I'd say we are not in the labour ward yet but thanks so much Donna.

I will see my darling Dad tomorrow and hold his hand and speak with my eyes, my heart, and my presence. There will be others visiting and I am gatecrashing, so I will be staying small because it's their time with him.

Words are so limited and unsatisfying at these times. They can get in the way. All the years we meditated together away at retreat, and in our homes are reaping a wonderful Harvest - just "being there" feels like a long, deep conversation.

I pray we will be able to keep those "silent chats" going, long after he leaves his costume behind and returns home to pure light.

Take some time to savour this Harvest Moon; reflect on and be grateful for all your blessings. It's all pure gift.

THE WISDOM OF MY FATHER

I thought I'd share some wisdom from my mentor/father today. I'm heading up to see him en route to the Meditation Retreat that Graham is leading up in Kinnoul this weekend. I'm ready for some silence and solitude up in the Pine Woods here after a busy weekend and crazy week! It's bittersweet though because Dad has been there for the last few years or so.

I've been quite aghast at the conduct of some "professionals" who know what's going down but have let ME down greatly, one after another - even tried to take advantage!

One in fact has let me down three times in a row within two weeks, by changing an arrangement at the last minute - once 30 minutes before the meeting.

It's something I want do for my dad while he is still able to appreciate it. He knows this, knows my father, and it's too late to go elsewhere. Time is at a premium.

I wish, dear reader, I could say that was all. But it's not, other let downs ensued. I know it's a Full Moon but do folk think yer daft?

I know the world is full of flawed human beings because I am one myself but I really do need to remind myself sometimes that (cue James Taylor...)

"When you're down, and troubled and you need some love and care, there's often some arsehole hanging about, ready to try to take advantage of you"

My father taught me well though. I have an extract from a draft of a speech he delivered to final year students at a prizegiving. He gave it to me on Monday and it's so fitting.

Perfect timing Dad, again.

THE MONK

When I planned to give a retreat for six women on Iona next weekend, nine months ago, I had no idea of how important it would be.

I am thirsty for the healing calm, the stormy rainclouds, and the dazzling sunrises. My heart is longing for time of solitary walks in the landscape that so soothes my soul.

My dad is stable for now, his pain levels reduced. Drug companies get a bad name these days but today I bless them.

He is a bit more mobile, eating little but eating again. I need to step back and give others more time to visit, and he wants some time to put affairs in order/see doctors, and have some "quiet time" too.

The Spiritual side of his Journey is expanding deep and wide - he shared some of it with us, for a while yesterday.

It was breathtaking. His face shone, his eyes sparkled and his voice deepened. Was it a trick of the light that I saw him "transformed" into a wee wise shaven-headed monk surrounded by light while he was telling us? I dunno, but I risked telling G on the drive home. He had had the same experience at the same time.

Dad finished "Ach, people will probably think I'm crazy!".

We don't.

DANCING WITH THE CAPTAIN

After a very full weekend of Reiki Teaching, I am off "Dancing With The Captain" today, as the old Paul Nicholas song said! I am Dad-sitting, so I get him mostly to myself ALL DAY. My niece and brother will pop up too.

I can't tell you how precious and valuable these minutes and hours are; they are sacred time.

I bathe myself in the light that surrounds him now - it is tangible and visible; it sings, it touches my heart every time.

We all have this light, we just need to raise our altitude, slow down and tune in long enough to see it, feel it, hear it - but, it's always there. My Dad's light body is getting stronger by the day as his physical body is fading - in direct proportion.

Today, we will cry, laugh, reminisce plan and fire-fight symptoms, and sit in silence.

The thing is you never know which visit may be your last.

I'm away to deliver a retreat on Iona on Wednesday, and back Tuesday to visit. Everyone, including Dad, says "Go, we are not there yet!" but there is always a lingering fear that if I'm more than a couple of hours away... let alone the six to Iona.

He wants me to go, so I will.

We both visited Iona for his 80th birthday gift from me, this time last year. He placed a stone on the Cairn in Sand Eel's Bay, and gave me one to place on it too, saying "This will always be here, for all time, to mark our being here together."

I want to sit by that Cairn and sing his funeral hymn to the sea: "There's a time to remember, there's a time to recall, the tears and the triumphs, the fears and the falls".

Sounds bloody depressing, but it cheers up in the chorus, honest.

Meanwhile I'm off to find Paul Nicholas singing that 70s hit on YouTube and have a wee jig as I get ready to visit my Captain. "So we all had fun the whole night long, as the ship sailed on".

TIGHNA

There's something about crossing water on a ferry that transports me on another deeper level.

I always feel as if I've crossed oceans and time zones when I come to my brother's place in Tighnabruach - yet it's less than a two-hour journey away.

Dad is adamant he doesn't want us around too much just now, and wants some free days for peace and contemplation.

I realised I needed some of that too, so we escaped here for a few days. Thanks Chris.

I have slept remarkably well recently, considering; though it may be just tiredness from driving cross country between Helensburgh (mum) and Perth (Dad) and Glasgow (Clinic) nearly every day.

With weekend training courses now re-commenced, the academic term has kicked off with big changes, and the inevitable hour long FaceTime calls with colleagues that ensue. I needed to STOP.

However, on Thursday night I was still awake at 2am and restless as the sea on a windy day.

So I got up, paced about like a hip hop dancer on speed, ate a mountain of Red Berry Special K with a litre of mega-fat milk from a trough; and succumbed to my phone for respite and distraction.

And there I found a late night posting of a message from a very dear soul friend (thanks Helen). Who has my back at this mystifying time? It was a beautiful prayer and part of a Novena (a prayer cycle) she is following. She was including me in it.

The jangling and clanging stopped in my head immediately.

I sat and watched the black clouds morph and mingle with the moonlight, and allowed the perfume of her prayer to permeate my being. I felt Connected. Soothed. Held.

I was then totally overwhelmed when, as I tried to turn off, I discovered a sponsored ad for a FREE Ram Dass video of his early talks.

One of Dad's favourite Spiritual writers, mine too.

So I watched the first. About watching life from various TV Channels/perspectives and how, when we watch from Channel 5, we come from the connected viewpoint and see the Big Picture.

With a full heart and eyes brimmed full and running over, I headed back to my nest.

These days, I really do feel as if I'm walking with one foot in the Material World, and the other in the "Invisible World" of synchronicity, shimmering  light and sharpened to a fine point intuition.

G is open wide too - yesterday he answered a question I was just about to ask him.

Either that or I'm on the slippery slope to the Very Special Section of the Hospital.

# CHAPTER 5:
# OCTOBER 2016

MESSAGE IN THE SAND

It's been a busy week, with a cold. Feels more like a cleansing but still an annoyance. I'm meeting myself coming back but strangely had booked some days off in the next two weeks, a few months ago, for no apparent reason. I'm glad of that now and after this certificate weekend, no more teaching weekends for a month.

I wanted to share a weird experience I had on Iona last Sunday. I sent the group off to do an exercise in solitude and silence in the stunning landscape, and I decided to join in. I headed down to the beach and noticed someone had written something on the sand in the distance. "Someone's love declaration to the heavens," I mused. "Probably Wullie loves Betty!"

I sat on the rocks and talked animatedly and frankly to God, and any other redundant angels or saints who may have been looking for some overtime.

"Guys, I'm getting a bit afraid of this next bit with Dad, for him mostly but for me and all of the family too. Any chance of a wee reassuring sign to remind me you have my back, and you're on the case? Sorry to ask but needs must."

Five minutes - nothing. Not a peep. Not a Jonathan Livingston Seagull doing a fly past; not a love heart-shaped cloud, not a damn ripple in the water that sounded like an angel singing. Nought. Nil points.

I hmmmmphed my way back up the beach to return back for the next group session, with a dejected air. As I walked I remembered that I had to send my email address to John so he could send the recording of my hymn for Dad's funeral and I absentmindedly mused that I should pop into St Mary's Church some time soon (never been in it in my life) to check out how/where an amplifier could be put to play it.

Don't ask me why I walked the longer way back up the beach, or why I stopped to read the "lover"s" inscription in the sand .....NOT!

It read:

"ST MARY'S
SEND LOVE
FROM IONA."

GEESE A BREAK

Wild geese fly in a V formation. Each bird flies slightly above the bird in front of him, resulting in a reduction of wind resistance. The birds take turns being in the front, falling back when they get tired. In this way, the geese can fly for a long time before they must stop for rest. When one goes down through illness or exhaustion, another goes down with him and waits, returning only to the group when the situation is resolved.

My father flew at the front of our flock most of his life and rarely "went down". It's our time now to take turns each, of holding the V for everyone.

We seem to do that naturally, without a huge debate. And we all need our turn of "dropping back" or even "dropping down to land" for a rest.

My job as a therapist has prepared me for holding the tension of another's pain and distress without allowing it to overwhelm me; and to delay the "gratification" of expressing my emotions/feelings until a later, more appropriate time, when necessary.

I've sat with a lot of people in a lot of pain these past 30 years in my work. And mostly, especially as I gained more experience, I've been able to "hold the space" for others without meltdown. However, this is no client; I need regular meltdown moments now.

But knowing when and how to drop back and descend to ground is crucial in order to be able to take my turn at the front.

Sleep has become a welcome friend. Being around cancer, death and dying, and supporting others in grief is an exhausting exercise. You need far more than normal.

Vitamins and minerals: nuts and seeds, alkaline water (water with squeezed lemon or bicarbonate of soda) to drink help replenish, rebalance and neutralise the acidity in the body from excessive prolonged stress/hyper-vigilance.

Cuddles and hugs: any time, anywhere - men /women /children/ babies/ cats/ dogs / strangers. Soak them up - they heal the daily paper cuts!

Silence - time for my soul to catch up with me, without my busy, arrogant, self-righteous, controlling left brain trying impotently to run the show all by itself.

And cinnamon balls!

Every one of us has become addicted to those childhood sweeties I place in a bowl by my dad's chair or bed. We try to talk with monstrous extended cheeks full of boiled sugar, mumbling sentences that need to be repeated to be understood. Hope no-one chokes to death, I'll get the blame. They are comforting anchors to our childhood; self-soothers. Solero ice lollies too.They should be given out on an NHS prescription, for dry mouth syndrome and just to make you smile with glee. My next "Healing the Inner Child" workshop will have a completely different slant and flavour!

And good movies/TV that transports me down to ground for an hour or two, where I can lose myself in the storyline. Girl on a train was one, and Bridget Jones' Baby - with G being the token man amongst 100 hysterical women - was another!

Folding laundry; washing dishes in the sink; these have become moments of stillness and reflection to still my chattering monkey mind.

But my most grounding and restoring times occur when I give my father a reflexology and leg massage, which he asks for every visit now. I work in silence - but everything is said. I am anointing him as I apply the oils and am reminded of the Sacrament of The Washing of The Feet. I am honoured and privileged to hold in my hands the world-weary and worn feet of my beloved dad - feet that have gone the distance of countless marathons around the world, literally, and metaphorically.

Feet that have kept going, no matter the pain or sacrifice involved, at times walking through Hell and back again, to provide for and protect me, my family and countless others over the years.

The same feet I used to practice dancing on as a child. My feet will never forget how to dance.. he taught me how.

A fitting time to give you my rewrite/reinterpretation of the great Ram Dass:

On Crossing The Veil :

Don't anticipate the future, don't regret the past.

Let go of it all with forgiveness.

A part of us dies at the end of this life; another part of us doesn't. Everything changes except your soul.

Get to know your soul, your ego will make itself known well enough.

There are dimensions other than the one we are aware of here .

There we will meet the souls that we met in our life, as just souls: we won't meet them as Mum, Dad, Gran or Papa.

This is a place of immense beauty beyond our wildest imagination: with colour and music and unconditional love at source.

This place is where it starts: the womb of the beginning of everything.

The Divine Creative Intelligence lives in the essence and heartbeat of this Place.

Dying is the most important moment in any life.

Don't be scared of your transition from here to the other side of the Veil: you will be surrounded and accompanied by a magnificent, deep, wide love that is so familiar - you will recognise exactly who is involved.

I wish you a peaceful transition

I wish you a Good Death.

I wish you the Love that will envelop you in that place of incredible light.

## CIRCLE OF WOMEN

I love this piece forwarded on by a good friend, Frances. I hope it resonates with you:

"I sit in circle with women, each one of us at a turning point and looking for guidance – something to direct us to the answers we seek, whose questions reside in numinous places, away from the structures, roles, and regulations of normal daily life. We are there to gain strength and resilience in a territory that we have been taught we have no business in: the territory of women's wisdom. Each woman holds a question on her heart and looks to the woman beside her or across from her for a morsel of reflected truth that is her own, spoken in a different voice, worn in a different skin, and yet, feels familiar.

Our paths are different, but in that room I am not alone. As one woman holds the talking stick, her voice shaking from her pain, tears spilling from her eyes, streaking down her face, a heat forms in the base of my spine. The words "I hear you" form inside me. My silent prayer is passed on to the woman across from me and yet, it is also meant for me, as each woman's journey to her deepest truth moves me closer to my own.

The tears are spilled and gathered in our circle – a sacred pool anointing our fear, our pain; gathering our courage, our hope. Our collective journey ebbs and flows as the circle continues, rounding out as the talking stick makes its way. But still, a silence wells within me – something not yet touched, not yet spoken. What am I protecting? What is safe to speak? I look around the room and my silence holds me just above the truth I've come so far to face. What would it mean to be fully seen?"

Written by Kristen Roderick

## BLACK SHOES

Practising Mindfulness is hard, living in the Present Moment, at the best of times. It can seem damn near impossible during the worst of times; the mind changes channel from The Past, to The Future, to The Now, to Inter-Galactic Time.

I was rebooking a client on Thursday for a bit ahead because of my dad's failing health. We booked in a few appointments, and as I wrote in one for the week before Christmas.. Boom! My legs nearly buckled. He won't be here. I KNOW this, but my body is playing keepy-up.

More intimate and bittersweet stories are shared by loving friends here and privately messaged.

They are heart-stretching, raw and honest. One shared beautiful memories of balloons and nightlights placed on her mother's coffin by the children.

I had been feeling guilty for fast-forwarding, realising I don't have any black shoes and black Jesus sandals (whilst being appropriate in one sense) probably wouldn't cut it.

I mused that a wee trip to The Fort Shopping Centre would be a good idea at some point.

Back and forth, vain attempts at a sense of CONTROL but I am powerless.

Others shared stories of bereft family members' power and stuff-grabbing.

Angry heated exchanges from relatives that shocked and ambushed them. All that ANGER flying around their loved and cherished family members.

It occurred to me that anger, and failed attempts at control, are simply grief in action.

Of course the anger had absolutely nothing to do with who got Granny's good pearls, or who was phoned first/last, or even who held a tassle at the graveside.

It's our old friend fear in action, dressed up as anger. The technical term is Displacement of Anger.

Of course what's really going down is anger at the person who died.

"How very dare he/she! How can you leave me like this?"

And then anger at God*/Life*/The Universe*/ Gaia*/The Mysterons*

(*Tick as appropriate.)

"How can you do this to me/them?"

And finally anger at ourselves for the regrets, mistakes, things said and unsaid.

"How could I have done that/said that?"

But the underpinning fear, that life is short and fragile, and I really have no power or control over it - no matter how many vitamins, massages, workshops, books I consume - is at the heart of the matter. So frail humans argue over Granny's watch/Grandad's pipe/ who gets a tassle, and so on and on, to displace the fear and fake control. Not TAKE. FAKE.

On a Zen Buddhist Retreat recently, a chant was recited before bedtime.-

"Let me respectfully remind you: Life and Death are of supreme importance. Time passes swiftly by, and opportunity is lost. Each of us should strive to awaken".

Then he scared the Beejesus out of me and shouted: "AWAKEN! This night your life is diminished by one day. Take heed. Do not squander your life!"

How you gonna "Awaken" today, and how you gonna show them you love them? Every last one of them.

DEEPER STILL

I slept last night at my Father's, with a baby monitor by my ear. Role reversal indeed. I listened to him breathe and shift while I meditated in the room across the hall. Sleep wasn't an option for me until he had settled and FB is a great comforter in the wee sma' hours when you are awake by yourself.

I had lots of twee sound bites to begin a post with: "It's such a privilege.."; "I'm honoured.."; "I'm ever so humbled..".

But I AM. It's a HUGE privilege! It's also a waking nightmare and if I could hand this one back, there are times I totally would. The SAS and Intelligence interrogators know the one way to break a prisoner and get them to spill the beans is to just "threaten" to inflict pain on a loved one.

Although he is not in pain (he calls it discomfort), dad is becoming a bit confused and disorientated at times. However it's unpredictable, and he is sharper than a scalpel most of the time. He still camps it up and gives us belly laughs. But just like Benjamin Button, he has aged about 20 years in just two weeks.

He is being stripped of all his strength and wonderful giving nature, and put firmly into the position of surrender to RECEIVE LOVE - unconditional love at that.

Loving care from strangers; wonderful district nurses; the lovely young chiropodist; the hearing aid man from Perth who dropped everything (including his day off) to do a house call tomorrow; Jonathan (the GP) who spent a full hour here last night at 6pm checking in on dad and Margaret and then was in first thing after a palliative team meeting to change meds; and Tanya the MacMillan nurse ("she's a cracker," he says).

Then there were deluges of loving care from his family and friends, beautiful loving words from cards and letters (some real surprises - things he had done but thought nothing of, that people had never forgotten).

Kindness seemed to be a recurring theme, followed by friendliness and laughter as joint runners-up.

My friend Caroline lost her Dad this week within a couple of days in hospital: his funeral is on Wednesday. Maureen buried her sister three weeks ago. We are all in this together. Michelle's mum has the same pancreatic cancer as dad - just a longer prognosis.

Here's all I know: suffering and illness can call forth the very best from us, if we allow it to. It's feckin' hard - but it takes us SO DEEP into the place inside we didn't know we had. I feel as if my rib cage has been expanded to make more space for my heart, because it's grown so big, too big to fit in that wee space any more. My heart is inflamed with love; love for this amazing, crazy journey we call life, for the raw and naked beauty of all of it and for people everywhere - those I know and even those I don't! My heart is going through "growing pains".

Love is in the soiled bed linen and clipping of finger and toenails; it's in the dishes and pans, boiling of kettles, the listening at doors for reassuring breathing. It's in the changing of light bulbs, fitting of hearing aid batteries.. and soon it will be in the bed baths and bedpans.

Love has no boundaries and it is the most precious and beautiful thing ever created. And you can dive as deep as you want to: it's all down to you.

I recently recorded a song for my brothers, If (When You Go) by Judy Tzuke, but it may be timely and healing for other family members and friends too, in fact anyone dealing with loss or grief.

You can hear me singing it at: https://youtu.be/0C-YSeYrLTY

LEARNING TO BE A GOOD LOSER
The first step in any 12-step addiction programme is "we admit we are powerless over alcohol/drugs/food/gambling /sex/ people".

Shame there isn't a Grief Anonymous group. "We admit we are powerless over death".

The problem with losing someone we love to a terminal illness, or any chronic illness for that matter, is you canny think your way out of it. You canny work harder on a solution, you canny find someone who can help you fix it/ has the answer/ knows a man.. You are POWERLESS. The ego takes a pounding on an hourly basis. The train is coming down the track and it gets closer every day. I wish it was over; then I catch myself mid-thought and know in my heart I don't want it to end.

I'm heading up to Dad's tonight and staying for a couple of days to give Margaret a break, and get out into the world for a while. I left some "space" yesterday for other family to visit without crowding him out.

Now it feels, when I'm leaving, that I have to peel myself away. When I'm at home, I jump whenever the phone rings. I long to get back.. then I dread the journey back up the motorway. It's all paradoxical.

However, once I'm there, I'm aware again of the light around him. It draws me in. I can see it, only when I don't look for it, but I can also feel it . And it calms me, soothes me; restores me. I know what needs to be done. I know it will all be okay, in the grand scheme of things.

"All shall be well, and all manner of things shall be well" - Dame Julian of Norwich. OMG, I'm even referencing properly now!

Rainbows have been a recent companion on the journey up and down the M80 to Gleneagles. They are like welcome friends these days, and are becoming my favourite colour.

Hope I don't start dressing like a PlaySchool presenter. To be honest, if the funeral dress code was up to me, I'd ask everyone to come dressed in rainbow colours or as clowns. That would be SO befitting my Dad's life. But methinks that'll be a "Naw!" from him.

I'm heading up to do the Nightwatch/Listen-in. He is deteriorating and very unstable on his feet. He will take to his bed any day now and sedation has already been mooted as an idea. He is already confused at times.The father I knew has already left the building in the past week or two; and a wobbly, stooped, soft, sleepy, slow-motioned Angel with slurred speech who sometimes talks in riddles has replaced him. I love him more than ever. The glimpses of his brilliant wit and humour are worth the wait and his feisty independence and stubbornness still put in an intermittent appearance - "I CAN GET IT!!!". Even though he clearly can't.

"I'm NOT an INVALID". Even though he clearly IS!

Offers of brain scans to see if it's spread there have been politely refused. Hospice respite too. Meds are being rearranged to remove any suspects in the recent confusion... you've got to LOVE our beautiful sweet amazing NHS and its lightworkers.

My Dad ran easily 30 plus marathons all over the world. He often talked about "THE WALL" that runners hit about the 21-mile mark, where all that keeps you going through the shutdown of your body, the confusion in your mind and the pain and cramping in your legs and hips, is the hours and years of training you have put in, and your mental attitude.

You just keep putting one foot in front of the other, ignore the thoughts in your head telling you that you can't go on, listen to the people cheering you on, and keep your eyes fixed on the finish line, once you can see it.

He said you always get a second wind when you least expect it and feel carried across that line. He was my coach, when I did my "equivalent" - a 10k years ago. He walked "Liz's Walk" (11+ miles with me, at MY pace this time last year, along the canal path to The Falkirk Wheel. Liz was my amazing pal who died of breast cancer last May.

I am cheering him all the way to the finish line at the start of the Rainbow Bridge, and I know Liz, Gran and Papi, Peter, my Emma and all his beloved friends and family will be there to cheer him across and welcome him somewhere on the other side of that rainbow.

# CHAPTER 6:
# NOVEMBER 2016

FALLING UPWARD

Last night my Dad had a fall during the night - the Marie Curie nurse couldn't prevent it, as he refused her access to the loo. Stubborn to the end.

But he is learning to receive and to accept help (busted nose and double bumped head notwithstanding).

Today, I gave him a manicure, and offered a pretty pink polish.. he refused vehemently and I can't repeat the words of his non-politically correct refusal here. But he did demand his reflexology, which he says is "soooooo relaxing and almost spiritual". That's because it's laced with Reiki, Dad.

He has fallen three times now in total, just like another lovable chappie who lived a long time ago. He still carries his cross with great dignity.

Every time, he rises; today saying "I'm going downstairs to have a change of scene and watch the REAL telly!" (It's got Netflix) and down the stairs he did go, after six tours of the bedroom to warm up his weary legs.

My time with him in silent reflexology is priceless - there are no words, but there is constant communication. I am so grateful that I trained in it over 30 years ago; even though I have never used it professionally.Nothing is ever wasted.

When I left him tonight, albeit reluctantly- as it ever is - he gave me a beaming smile, or was he just enjoying the Soor Ploom sweetie he was sooking? It doesn't matter.

## PURE LOVE

Leaving my Dad tonight, as he lay in bed (he is very weak and groggy), he asked me to say a prayer for him. I told him I didn't think he needed them, that he is and always has been pure love, but I would do what he asked. I told him many of us were praying for him. He smiled and seemed to like that idea.

## THE VEIL

My Dad passed over the Veil at 6pm tonight. All of your love, prayers and Reiki created a vortex of light around him such that he simply slipped SOOOOOO peacefully; just didn't take another breath. The last sound from him was a hearty "HA!". How very, very typical of my Dad.

We were truly blessed in that we had been with him all day, and we were with him when he stopped breathing.

He looked beautiful and radiant and his eye (only the left one was open) was transfixed on the corner of the ceiling. I asked "Do you see someone there Dad, have they come to help you?" He looked through me, intently at that corner. Five minutes later he was gone.

We had just been listening to his songs, Smile, Though Your Heart Is Aching and I Get A Kick Out Of You, then RIGHT on the last note, he kicked off.

My uncle blessed him (my uncle is a priest) half an hour before he passed.

You guys have been true Soul Friends these last four months. Thank you, thank you.

Pray for Patrick Trainer RIP.

I feel tremendously lucky, carried and grace-filled and don't doubt that I will come down at some point and perhaps crawl around the carpet for a while, but for now I am truly blessed. Love you, my Captain.

## FOR HYMN·

A bit early, but I'll be busy early doors. I thought I'd share my hymn which I will sing, albeit pre-recorded, at Dad's funeral.

Some friends and family won't make it on Friday so you can have a wee greet too. Why should I be the only one? You can hear the hymn on YouTube, just go to: https://youtu.be/uyoxjC86ASo. It's called There Is A Place.

THE OLD MONK

One day during the summer, my dad was telling us how surrounded he felt by "a loving, compassionate aura with the familiarity of loved ones". A very spiritual feeling he couldn't articulate with words. He restated this several times over the coming weeks.

He had no fear of what lay beyond the Veil because of this supportive "Field of Grace"; he just didn't fancy the dying thing itself. During this chat, I noticed a trick of the light and saw his face morph several times into that of an elderly monk type figure in robes. How the mind can play tricks, eh?!

On the way home, I risked being sectioned and told Graham. He confessed to the same experience at exactly the same time. At least we would share a ward in Leverndale!

The image of the Old Monk stayed with me, and during a treatment with a therapist friend, I noticed she had a photo on her wall of her Buddhist teacher.

My Dad was very interested in and open to ALL religions/philosophies if they originated in love.

The photo looked very familiar, even though I was looking at it upside down, as I lay there on the massage couch. It looked remarkably like the monk I had seen as my eyes "played tricks", that day during the summer.

One of the first condolence cards was from that therapist - she met dad only once, a year earlier, when Dad and I were away together. For only our second trip together alone in my 56 years. Strange? Never!

CONSCIOUS GRIEVING

And so, the work of conscious grieving begins.

Anticipatory grief, from watching terminally ill family/friends, the slow fading of dementia, or just plain old age creeping in on our loved ones certainly gives us a head start on it. But I know too that there is a deep dig ahead. No-one can protect us from it; no-one can do it for us.

Finding those last texts, seeing old videos/photos, absent-mindedly saying "wait till I tell dad about that!" rips the freshly formed scabs from the wounds on a daily basis.

There is no doubt that the love, caring, prayers, Reiki and blessings from others surrounds and sustains us. Well, for a while. THEN the journey ahead begins. Alone.

I'm a lucky girl - I have good loving people who have my back. I did plan, and am taking time off now until New Year. Not everyone can do this. How folks with young kids/shift work/aging parents do this I simply do not know. I will still have responsibilities to deal with. I will call regularly and often, and have to pop in to the clinic now and again. But I know I NEED time now.

There is a darkness ahead that I want to embrace. John of The Cross talked of "The Dark Night of The Soul."

I'm going to walk a beach at St. Andrews tomorrow with my G, sit by a log fire and drink nice wine, eat fish, and sleep in a cosy hotel with warm fluffed-up towels, and plan this precious time.

Already I feel called to the island of Iona for some solitude and to visit the cairn where Dad and I left pebbles last year. G will come for a few days, and then head home. Some things need alone time.

I want to write a letter to my Dad, expressing any unfinished business, hurts, fears, anger, regrets, frustrations, love, joys, memories, gratitude....ALL of it. Then I will read it to the sea and burn it on the beach at the North End.

I want to sit amongst the candles and talk to him, to pray, to cry openly and abundantly.

I want to sleep until I'm spent, walk in the wind and eat Sr. Jeans pavlova until I'm stuffed.

I want to walk and hear his voice in the wind.

On my return, I plan to visit his childhood streets, our childhood homes, his special places. I want to photograph some of these places maybe for a calendar. I want to write him a poem, or even a song.

Maybe then I'll be ready to be with my friends who have patiently stepped back to give me the kind of space they know I need.

G and I plan to set off for Lindisfarne (Holy Isle) the week before Christmas to avoid the Spendfest frenzy. Pat, like us, loved it there too in Dark Winter, when the seas cover the causeway and transform it into a magical island again. There is only ONE Christmas tree there. Hurrah!

Then, I hope I can return and hold this Christmas gently, with its welcome return of the light into the world. Maybe I can then, after the new start of the New Year, handle taking up the reins of a busy Clinic. The work I love, but can't contemplate at the moment.

I know that a month of conscious griefwork is only the start of the "marathon" of loss of a parent; but it's preparation and training for the long walk ahead. It's finding that rhythm. One breath at a time, one step at a time.

God bless you Dad, leave a light on in Heaven for me. I love you. x

THE PROTECTIVE AURA

It feels all uphill, but Jeezo it's only day four after the funeral.

Dad had talked of the "protective aura around him, of "invisible friends, grace and love" carrying him forward.

I know what he meant now. The love, shared wisdom, cards, flowers, kind offers, gifts, beautiful words and prayers of friends and heart/blood family are carrying ME now.

There is often a backstory at these difficult times, the undertow. After all, we are dealing with human beings on these journeys. And my situation is no different.

There have been "difficulties" and issues that have to be acknowledged, felt and worked through, now that Dad is at peace. This is not the forum to discuss, but let's just call it "The Keegh".

It awakens me in the morning, the unfinished business that may never get closure. Things said, unsaid, heard; should I have done more, less, nothing when boats were rocking and threatening to sink?

A good friend suggested I "hand it all over to God", and I try. But God seems to hand a fair bit of it back, and says, "you need to sift through some of this "keech" first to find the nuggets of gold in there, the learnings, the wisdom - nothing is wasted".

I know that now my father knows the whole story, the big picture, and can read my heart. I know what my motivations were and I also know that not everyone sees the world the way I do. Shame, that. Life would be so much easier if they did.

And so the work begins of sifting through the messy stuff, so I can find my bearings again.

G has been like my walking poles, supporting and steadying me on the way. Always a hand on my back; just there. Dad introduced us - he'd known G for eight years before we actually met. I wonder if he knew how much I'd need him one day.

Thank you to all of you for your amazing support. You will probably never know how much it means.

# CHAPTER 7:
# DECEMBER 2016

A STRANGE DAY

Breathing underwater.

It felt more like a jammies day but I was persuaded to go into the clinic and collect my abandoned car from last night's revelries. So I did.

I had a wee meltdown, realising that Dad would never see the "new-look clinic" in person and my G held my hand while I warbled like a Christmas Turkey realising it was December.

Shirley, the resident Clinic Angel in human dress, flew about in reception and came in when I was "composed" with the daily updates. I saw a familiar name on the call-back list. An old boyfriend from well over 20 years or so. He'd heard.

To call or not to call?

I did.

I'm so glad I did. This relationship did not end well, and there was no closure. Despite living in the same city, we'd never once bumped into each other in over 20 years.

What followed was a beautiful healing and reminiscence of times with my Father. He was sad to have heard of the funeral too late. I never thought, nor had contact info.

But what mattered was his heartfelt apology and ownership of our parting.

He gave me bits of myself back again.

I can't explain it all - but I knew my Dad was in on it somehow. I tried to help my parents get closure, at dad's request, before Dad died. And, of a fashion, they did .

He recounted his appreciation of my "idiosyncrasies" (by the way, he is in a happy relationship... just sayin'!) and much more than owned his "stuff".

I got the chance to own mine too, those unaware, hitherto unexpressed things.

It was a beautiful moment, on a mobile, in a car park, of deep healing of unfinished business. Thanks Dad.

THE ROBIN

Laura went off and looked up the animal totem meaning of the robin after my encounters with them over the last couple of days. Here is the start of her reply, and the pic is the cover of my Dad's autobiography. Coincidence? Of course not!

"I found this Angela: 'If a robin has flown into your life; robin signifies stimulation of new growth and renewal in many areas of life. He teaches that any changes can be made with joy, laughter and a song in your heart'."

Love, love, love.

FINDING THE GLORY AGAIN

After a nine-hour journey back to my Mother's last night, I took the long road home via the Schoenstatt Chapel which nestles in the foot of the Campsie Hills. It is a place of great tranquility and beauty.

I found the transition from Iona back to the reality of the Christmas Spendfest shoppers in Oban, with all their inherent expectations, a strange one.

I really have no interest in it this year at all. Does that make me a Scrooge?

My mum's tree is up - we helped put it up, but I felt nothing this year as I looked at it.

Of course I faked enthusiasm. Some say you've got to fake it to make it. I don't know.

For the first time personally, I really got how tough these times of celebration are for those who have lost family around this time of year, or during the year.

It's difficult to find the balance between engaging for the greater good of those around us, yet not denying our own feelings which, if squashed, will only bite us on the bum further down the road. But I don't want to do a "Bah, humbug!" either.

Everyone is affected when a family member passes, not just us. All of my family are struggling with the same - and different - tumultuous emotions. And there are children who need to be considered. And it's Christmas.

Maybe the wee Christmas story itself helps. The Child was born not in a beautiful palace or magnificent castle - so the story goes - but in a shitty, smelly, old dilapidated stable in the muck and dust.. and glory.

The place where nobody would choose to be.

Maybe, when we have loved and lost, the Light returns exactly there, in the smelly old stable, in the broken place within the heart.

The place where nobody would choose to be. The place you will find the glory again.

PAYING IT FORWARD

To start 2017 off in a loving way I'm participating in the Pay It Forward initiative. The first five people who comment on this status with "I'm in" will receive a surprise from me at some point in 2017 - anything from a book, a ticket, something home-grown or made, a postcard, absolutely any surprise. There will be no warning, it will happen when the mood comes over me and I find something that I believe would suit you and make you happy. These five people must make the same offer in their Facebook status and distribute their own joy. Simply copy this text on to your profile (don't share), so we can form a web of connection and kindness. Let's do more kind and loving things for each other in 2017, without any reason other than to make each other smile and show that we think of each other.

HELL AND HEAVEN

Christmas without my Dad around was tough but do-able; with

chunks of solitude, good pacing, a lot of prayer and support when needed, I got through it.

It was made tougher by background "stuff" that I didn't foresee in a month of Tuesdays. But it's stuff good friends and a husband who have been on the road before me tell me is fairly normal and typical, though with my lowered immunity to life, it felt anything but.

So with my fingernails dug into the kitchen table, I hung on for our escape to Iona Island for New Year. We were SUPPOSED to be leaving on the 29th for five nights. To boot we let a friend's daughter and pal have our house for New Year after their heating broke, and couldn't be repaired until January 4th, and they could catsit Ian too. Great plan!

Then on Wednesday morning we discovered due to adverse winds there were no ferries to Iona for two days or more, and Jean (our host) cancelled her return too.

I spent five hours on Google looking for a rural cottage with fire and sea/loch/river anywhere in Scotland. All booked out, of course. Only the wee dumps left on the books at crazy prices.

I decided to book into Leverndale Hospital for a Valium cure over Hogmanay.

Lord Graham, of course, went for a two-hour walk, saying before he left "Don't worry - it'll be fine!"

You can imagine my expression.

When he returned, he fiddled on the laptop, and 30 minutes later.. Abracadabra! We got a last minute cancellation, at a reduced rate. The loch, the mountains, no cottage or fire but a beautiful self catering apartment in a glorious position near Schiehallion (The Fairy Mountain) which I've wanted to visit for two years.

The moral of the story: it helps if you're in the zone and at the right altitude when you are asking the Universe for help. Raise your altitude! When you're stuck in the mud, don't keep churning the wheels - take a break, put your wellies on and go for a walk until the rain goes off. And then, try again.

And remember to say thanks.

THANK YOU, WE ARE VERY GRATEFUL!

2016: THE LAST POST

Would I change a thing? Probably not.

It's all a beautiful quilt of light, shade, dark and vibrant colour.

This year, I learned more and grew more through the suffering and the tight places than I did on any of the sunny days and beach holidays of the past.

My heart was opened and stretched to the max and through that I discovered depths within me I didn't know existed. I discovered a fearless courage inside of me, a desire for truth and honesty I couldn't hold back on, an ability to laugh in torrential rain, a connection with everyone and everything that nearly blew my circuits.

I have a hunger to be fully ME, with whatever time I have left on this amazing planet.

When the shit hit the fan, and it DID more than once, there was a lot of compost created for future harvests.

Love hurts - it's the price we pay. And Love NEVER dies.

I wish you a New Year filled with hope and strength; a strong inner compass set to your truth. A year of heart-opening, with liberal doses of joy and laughter. I love you all. And love never dies. x

# CHAPTER 8:
# JANUARY 2017

POSTCARDS FROM BEYOND

My First Foot this morning was a beautiful robin. First time out the front door, second time out the back door 10 minutes later. Happy New Year from Heaven? I like to think so.

I kept all the 36 cards I had sent to my Dad during his five months of illness; each had a lovely memory or a funny story we'd experienced, and some simply had expressions of love in them.

I brought five, chosen at random, away with me here to Kenmore. One for each day.

As I got into bed at 2am I chose one, again randomly, for New Year's Day. The last words I had written in it were "Love Never Dies".

That's exactly what I wrote to end my posting here on FB yesterday, "Love Never Dies".

I'm away for a lie doon!

DIVINE TIMING

Schiehallion is delayed until tomorrow due to blizzard conditions. Well, some snow and I was driving. So Fortingall Yew Tree (oldest living thing in the world) beckoned instead.

The hotel was closed for lunch but they were clearing away the guest buffet and let us at it. It was wonderful - food for at least 40, but only eight had turned up.

Divine timing again.

We passed some beautiful scenery and houses, apart from the spooky house! It had creepy energy galore.

Lazy TV night - but a cheeky wee prosecco left in fridge. Be a shame to waste it, right?

So beautiful up here. Don't come - you'd hate it (and it'd get busy, and we'd miss out on last minute cancellations). It's awful. Honest.

WHY I'M HERE

Preparing to teach the final weekend tomorrow of the post-grad students course. Treating depression is one of the major topics. And infertility to boot!

I haven't taught a group in two months, and only started seeing clients yesterday so the butterflies were abundantly fluttering through my gastro-intestinal system.

At first I thought, "what on earth am I doing? I must be nuts".

I'm struggling myself, at times in a fog of grief. Tears are often surprisingly closer than I'd prefer. And some days I awaken with a wall of cotton wool between me and the world, that can take until lunchtime to unpack.

I remind myself it's only been weeks since we buried my Dad. How soon is too soon; how long is too long?

So there I am, sitting in the hairdresser's chair, getting my roots brought into line with the rest of my goldilocks, when Caroline (my hair angel) asks how it all played out after the funeral. She then goes on to ask why I'm reading books on depression - am I depressed? I explain.

She tells me of her sadness and grief after her father died the year before and how she is still affected by bouts of mourning and melancholia.

When she concludes, I find myself delivering a mini-lecture on the stuff I'm presenting tomorrow.

When I finish, she smiles and says "I'm so glad you came in today - I had been struggling over Christmas and New Year, but you've given me a new perspective on my feelings; and I'm going to apply what you've taught me. I should be paying YOU today. Thank you!".

And as I leave, feeling a good six inches taller, with shinier hair, I am reminded of why I am here.

## CLOSING THE CIRCLE: THE FINAL CHAPTER

I can't really discuss here why, or express how much your beautiful birthday messages meant so much to me. People vilify Facebook: but truly, every single message touched my heart deeply.

I am living in strange times, in a foreign land that at times feels more like Blunderland than Wonderland but is equally as crazymaking.

But let me tell you a wee story of today.

After a magical weekend of fun and festivity with my darlin' man, we decided to revisit St. Mary's Cathedral before we left Edinburgh.

Some of you may remember that my journey with my dad began in June at St. Mary's Cathedral when he asked G and I to join him there, during a trip for my birthday gift from January, to see Chicago. He wanted us both to go light a candle with him and meditate together. We had initially indicated we needed a wee rest and cuppa but he called us on the phone to repeat his request.

It was then I told G I thought he was "dying".....though he wasn't diagnosed for another month.

I cried silently through the meditation, I just "knew".

Today we returned there to end our trip. I was nervous, but thankfully again wept silently, not noisily. I felt his presence beside me and lit another candle, this time with a different and more current intention.

I just "know " he is grand, and doing just fine.

It's those of us left behind who need the prayers.

The same wee priest who had come through the side door into the St. Mary's last June, did so again. Remarkable. Pin back yer lugs though, because he took the cover off the Baptismal Font and tried five times to light the large Paschal Candle, with no joy. It blew out, taper fell in half, blew out again. I thought, "that's my Da havin' a laugh!" and I know I was right. We laughed.. even the priest!

I said, "Better go G! Christening happening soon".

Smiley priest said, "No rush, be 10 minutes or so."

We sat quietly. He returned. We made to leave.

He said: "Would you be willing to be Surrogate Godparents to the child coming? The family are from Colombia and have no-one to stand for the boy."

There were two children being baptised: the Colombian toddler, in simple jeans but with a white shirt, accompanied by only his mum, dad and brother - all in anoraks. We looked a bit "windswept" by now ourselves - especially as I forgot to bring a comb or brush away.

The other child was bedecked in the finest finery with a family cast of dozens, groomed to the hilt. Of course we agreed.

Jared was good as gold. We made our responses heartily, held the candle and offered the white scarf - which he didn't fancy at all.

I took some photos and offered to email. They hadn't thought to bring a camera.

Later I told the parents why we were there. The priest hovered, so I shared with him. I said, "It felt like a closure and a new beginning. Love moves in mysterious ways".

His eyes filled as he said: "It's like a Circle of Life".

We hugged, the priest and I. We both wept quietly, as I said "Love NEVER Dies".

Got the title of the book, then.

And yes, as I write, the theme from The Lion King IS actually playing on Classic FM.

A WEE THINGY

Phew! Sometimes you just don't admit how scared you are until it all blows over. Still canny believe I kept this one to myself.

I had a wee "thingy " growing on my hairline behind my ears, I'm prone to wee skin tags, so didn't think much of it.

"WHAAAAAAT?!", I hear you say, given my dad's journey home started with a facial skin cancer.

Thankfully my hairdresser didn't take the same short-sighted view a couple of weeks ago, and commanded "You get that checked, now!".

Then G commented on my rather fetching ponytail with a "what the Beejesus is THAT thing growing out of your neck? You get that checked, NOW!"

So I did. And after weeks of worry, I was reassured today by the Doc that it was just a cyst (benign growth to you and me) and it was duly zapped away.

Don't be like Angie, be sensible. Get these things checked right away.

WALKING WITH PATRICK

Revisiting the North End Beach on Iona; where I walked last time with my Dad. Poignant, painful and panoramic... Patrick. Alliteration all the way, Ps galore.

I miss him so much. I think I've been pretending to myself he has been away on holiday for a month or so - like he used to in January - and he will be back soon.

But the beauty of the landscape enfolded me in its loving arms, while the birdsong and ballet of the crows enraptured my senses. And yes, I passed a field full of wild geese walking in both directions, there & back.

Night Dad, love you. Night all.

WHAT WOULD BUNNY SAY?

I'm in bed today, pole-axed.

I wrestled with myself all morning: got up, lay down, got up again, brushed my teeth, sat on top of the bed, dialled the clinic to cancel clients, changed my mind, hung up and got dressed, got undressed, lay under duvet, called clinic again, cancelled.

Got the picture? Of course, I shouldn't be exhausted/weak/done in, I just arrived back from four days on Iona last night! How can this be so?

But I am. I felt as if I had run into a brick wall when I arrived home after travelling for 11 hours; albeit with a pit-stop at Mum's.

I heard Martha Beck speak recently about EGO: two mice in a goldfish bowl, scrabbling and sliding on the inside of the glass trying to escape - like hamsters on a wheel - one white and one grey.

White Mouse: "I can and I will. Must try harder. Gotta get outta this damn goldfish bowl. Come on, move it, faster" as the wee beastie scrabbles away to no avail.

Grey Mouse (Self-Loathing - also Ego): "I hate myself, I'll never be able to get outta this damn bowl. I'm a lousy, useless piece of shit", as he scrabbles away to no avail.

And this dance goes on inside of us, all of our lives, unless we learn how to surrender to love. I need to observe the mice in the bowl, the internal struggle and overcome the voices of disappointment, in fact SHAME, that I am not "in control" at the moment.

My body is saying no. I am feeling weak, powerless and vulnerable and it's cost me my physical strength today.

I need to step back, rest, realign, regroup. It may take hours, days or even weeks. But total surrender is required. I have "prior/previous", as they say. I know what's needed here. My soul is playing catch-up.

Sir Ian is curled beside me vibrating his Reiki Purrs through the duvet. The ticking clock transports me back to my Gran's flat in Partick - a Healing Temple with scones. The thick white cloud I see through my window is like a soft fluffy baby blanket surrounding the house - cushioning me from the business and noise of the outside world.

I don't need potions or pills. Deep rest is all. It's been a busy six months of fulfilling all diary demands, even with lots of pit-stops to counter, and I'm done in!

I took a photo on Iona of a book. It made me smile.. my Dad's alter-ego was named Bunny from Landan, Eton-educated, who worked in the City - big eyes, buck teeth, cut-glass accent and slicked-back hair. A gin 'n' tonic kinda guy. We had some laughs at Bunny's commentaries on events in our lives. I'd ask: "What would Bunny say?".

Today Bunny would say "Don't be a mouse Daaaahling! Not a white mouse, not a grey mouse. Fiddlesticks to that! Have a duvet day and a cup of Earl Grey. And remember to breathe."

Tomorrow is another day....."

# CHAPTER 9:
# FEBRUARY 2017

WOBBLY WEEK

Full moons without doubt affect us all, especially when we are open and attuned to our senses - whether it be through the seasons, landscape or skies. And full eclipses are especially powerful. The word "Lunatic" comes from the Latin luna meaning Moon; the ebb and flow of tides are controlled by the position of the moon and our brains are around 75 per cent fluid so it figures, there is a pull on our inner tides too.

There are chemicals present in emotional tears which are not present if our eyes simply water for a physical reason. There are also some links between headaches/migraines and our inability to cry openly.

A good psychiatrist friend of mine once said "If we all had a good greet a couple of times a week, the drug companies would be out of business for sleeping pills, anti-depressants and tranquilisers."

I've been laid low by a virus this week and very weepy to boot. I decided to Let it Flow, and flow, and flow.

And my God, there were buckets, in fact BARRELS of tears.

Some recent issues of abandonment and that old chestnut betrayal rolled around again. These are the ones we can NEVER escape - which need to be faced head-on.

However, a bloody good greet does help pave the way; and cleans the pipes out from some of the old sediment of the past abandonments and betrayals.

I've experienced quite a few though, in recent months, since my father's death.

Going back further, however, my first husband calmly walked out the door between the starter and main course one night. I thought he was in the loo. I was 23 at the time, and it was, co-incidentally enough, in FEBRUARY 1983. He simply left and never came back. He did write, which was hugely magnanimous of him, however with no forwarding address. I didn't set eyes on him again until the night before our divorce two years later, when I wore my fur jacket, diamond earrings, best dress and heels, pretending I was en route somewhere amazing after our meeting. NOT back to my flat to howl, roar and greet on the carpet for hours. We'd been married nine months. He was engaged to a work colleague within a year or so.

So abandonment and I are dancing partners.

Betrayal and the loss of trust: well that goes back way much further, and is far too loaded for this particular forum. One day, maybe I'll write that book and the words "pigeons" and "cat" come to mind as I say that.

But no-one escapes these nut-crackers. Abandonment and betrayal. No-one.

And it is worth remembering, WE do our fair share of dishing it out too; if we are willing to reflect back for long enough.

So when the scabs of the old wounds are knocked off by current events and "assholes" ('scuse me for being judgemental) here in the present day, what do we do ?

When the tears flow - we let them.

Nobody has "crying" written as their cause of death on their Death Certificate.

Being weak and vulnerable through illness forced me to tap into a reservoir of tears that had been lying dormant, just waiting for release.

And it is the love of others that dries those tears and brushes them away.

Mr G with his timely hugs, cups of tea, setting fires and "just sitting there". Mr Ian the cat and his hot water bottle impersonations, purring, VIBRATING on my chest/belly/back/wherever he can climb on board!

My intuitive pal L, who has known me for 45 years, who broke her holiday and phoned from The Canaries for "a wee chat" and offered to research holiday accommodation for us out there for March.

Sister Jean (Spiritual Guide and Soul Friend aka Anam Cara) who texted from her retreat to say she had lit a candle for me, out of the blue.

And sometimes there's nothing else for it but to go make a big pot of homemade cream of celery soup and a big dish of homemade mac cheese and chorizo.

What do they say again? "Feed a cold, feed a virus, in fact feed a Full Moon Eclipse".

CUT THE CORDS

Today was a day for clearing out.. thoughts, feelings and people.

Some things had been "sticking in my craw", as my granny used to say.

I had taken a few "silent assassin" below-the-belt punches this past week, and in fact the last couple of months, but they were delivered with a smile and a hapless shrug; a kind of "whoops-a-daisy". You know the kind of thing dear reader, I'm sure you do.

I did reflect over many hours if I was being unreasonable in my expectations; a tad too controlling? Were my standards simply set too high in thinking that I deserved some common courtesy, from someone with whom I've had a 20-year-plus business relationship; in believing that telling the truth, and not "stealing" from me is a reasonable expectation?

In another friendship, when someone admits they have been careless to you, and they commit to making a renewed effort in the relationship, you would think they would actually have a go at that and not just do the same thing again. The thing that caused the pain in the first place!

So today, I put my thoughts in writing to both. I cut the cords that bind.

Why in writing? Because I really wanted them to read, and re-read what had taken me so long to figure out, and perhaps think twice for the future with someone else. The words "breath", "hold", "your" and "don't" all spring to mind though.

I have a long rope, mostly. But something has changed inside these past few months. I have realised how short life is, and how little time I have for pretence and mind games. And for people who aim water pistols up yer back, and tell you it's raining. Well, it's a politer version.

It is not so much what my fellow humans have done/not done, that mattered so much. It is the fact that they seemed to expect me to smile back, and thank them for the insult to my intelligence.

To keep things "nice". They mistook "SAFT" for "DAFT".

It was time for a wake-up call. And I am waking up big time now.

Wayne Dyer once said "Would you rather be right or would you rather be kind?" I once met someone who knew him VERY well, as a personal friend. It seems he wisnae always so hot at giving the right answer to that one himself. We are all only human.

So, Wayne, my answer is I'd rather be able to look myself in the mirror in the morning and say, "Precious goods on board this train - it's my job to take care of them."

There are more choices than "right" or "kind." And kind to who, exactly?

Yes, as long as I'm included in the kindness factor, I'll be kind to me, and give the gift of honesty at the same time.

Take those door jams oot, warrior woman a-comin' through.

LETTING GO OF THE ROPE

A friend of mine has been deeply hurt to find out that someone she knows has deliberately withheld possession of a treasured and irreplaceable item of her daughter's, who passed some years ago. I shared an experience of mine, in solidarity, to hopefully give her some comfort. It seems it is a more common occurrence than we may like to think, from some shared conversations I've had with people who have loved and lost.

We'll call her Betty....

Betty, this may be of absolutely no consolation whatsoever BUT I too found myself in a similar position. Someone had something of mine, given to me by G, as a gift.

I had lost possession of a very sentimental item - worthless to anyone else but priceless to me.

I had a long and difficult wrestling match with this situation in my head, and my heart. I finally found peace when I realised it wasn't about the "stuff". I have a hoose-ful, I REALLY don't need any more.

I was willingly participating in a tug-o-war, that would only end when I let go of my end of the rope. So I did. I detached.

I have always loved the story of the wise woman who has the beautiful diamond. Her student approaches, with a green glint in her eye and announces: "I really, really want that diamond. Give it to me!"

Wise woman: "Here, take it", and gives it to her.

Two weeks later the student comes back and hands back the diamond, saying: "I don't want the diamond, please have it back. I want to have whatever you have, that made you able to give it away."

I want that too. Sleep tight, dear friends.

# CHAPTER 10:
# MARCH 2017

PLAYING MY SONGS

I'm on holiday in Costa Adeje.

I wanted to be a music therapist when I was younger, but I wasn't good enough - I started too late to get the First Class Honours I needed to get into the Guildhall. So I settled for a degree in psychology and music and after sacking the notion of being a music teacher I worked in advertising for five years.

Life had other plans. Through a short-lived marriage, a broken heart which medicine calls depression, and a period of time with a great psychotherapist, I ventured out on the path of therapy training myself. That was all over 30 years ago. And as they say, the rest is history, and the Harvest Clinic was born.

And the music? It remained a hobby, an outlet, a release from the rigours of working with life-weary, broken and struggling people for hours every week.

But music was my first love. Allegedly, I introduced my parents to the music of the Beatles around the age of five-ish. Music heals. It stimulates the soul; awakens the heart.

I use a lot of music in my Reiki trainings, and other workshops and retreats; it always "reaches the parts" like a big glass of Heineken.

This weekend, a colleague who is very psychic but flies under the radar, shared that she "saw" my Father (who we nicknamed The Captain throughout his short illness) and Liz (my pal who died a few years ago) debating whether I should "play my songs" on guitar or piano.

Liz was a keen guitarist, Dad a fab jazz piano man. My psychic friend wasn't to know that I play both - though the guitar is very rusty. She also wasn't to know that I had let my music slide over Jan/Feb as I was blind-sided by a rip-tide of deep sadness, a month or so after my Father died, and by the realisation that my Dad was in fact NOT on one of his extended overseas holidays, and that he WASN'T coming back this time with great stories and good laughs.

She added that they said I should start on "my book". I guess she meant the one I started and then shelved. I suppose I shouldn't have been surprised when I awoke today, to find myself humming and singing a tune without words as I cleared up last night's dishes. I noticed and wondered what it was. I was only singing sporadic words unconsciously, so I let myself fill in the blanks .

"And we all had fun, the whole night long. And the Ship sailed on..Everybody was..DANCING WITH THE CAPTAIN".

Happy Monday! I'm off to play the piano and sing for a bit.

ON BOREDOM

I photographed the resident black swan yesterday and looked up its meaning: it allegedly signifies an "unforeseen event" and is also a messenger of spiritual love and freedom. It was.

I first noticed my twitchy feet in the morning. I had managed to stub my toe on a sunbed so wobbling my feet about was not my best move.

Then the fidgety, edgy, restless feelings surfaced. I was BORED in paradise. I wanted to be somewhere else; do something else, but WHAT?

How spoilt and ungrateful, I hear you say, dear reader.

Boredom is often a harbinger, for attempts at distraction; from the uninvited, unwelcome feelings that will follow. But if we will only sit still for long enough, we gain access to what lies beneath it. Foreboding low grade irritability and vague feelings of anxiety began rise to the surface, on this occasion.

Was it the heat? Hormones wobbling? I felt it was probably time to just sit, wait, see. There are a lot of older people here at this time of year; and many tall, white-haired, smartly-dressed men with side-sheds and sunglasses. From the back, on several occasions I've "seen" my father. Of course it's never him. But still, I'm entranced - just in case.

I realised, as I sat there, that in my joy and pleasure of being on holiday I hadn't cried for nearly a week. "Result," I thought. As I tried to breathe and lean into the tension in my diaphragm, the "boredom" dissolved.

When we stop, really STOP, that's when the uninvited guests make an appearance at our back door, catching us unaware. That's why we get so busy when we are grieving. We resist the stopping.

"Oh No. Sad and Grief just pulled into the driveway - quick, pull the curtains - pretend I'm out!"

Too late, they're both waving in the window shouting "Cooo-Eeee", and peeping around the doorway. Nothing for it but to welcome them in, put the kettle on, pull up a couple of chairs and settle in for a catch up. Be rude not to.

Sadness and loss get a bad press. They are just feelings after all. But we tell such big stories about them. Greeting by the pool in bright sunshine, in Paradise, may seem unconventional but I'm sure I'm not the only one here, teary-eyed behind my fake Ray-Bans. There will be other souls around the gardens and beach with diagnoses, prognoses, loved ones recently lost, divorces and estranged families.

They too will be smiling under their sun hat brims to the waiters, greeting them with a cheery "Hola!". My silent tears released the tension inside. Later, back in the room, G just held me as I cried for a long time, wordlessly.

I miss my dad, is all. Even yet, I can't quite take it all in. If I ever will.

It passed, a long bath helped. A quiet dinner and an early night were in order.

Strangely, we both dreamt last night about the same people and our dreams had a similar theme. G is grieving too. I also need to to remember that.

Today is a new day. I am no longer "bored". I am more in tune with my two old pals who arrived yesterday - sadness and loss. I'm taking them for a swim in the pool. Joy and laughter will no doubt join us there. Come on in, it's splashin'

## THE CAPTAIN RETURNS

I decided to use the Notes App on my phone to write. I have absolutely no recollection of using it before but I found a piece there yesterday. I guess I "must" have saved it somehow. But I didn't write it, and I don't remember saving it.

We came to La Gomera as a sort of pilgrimage - my Dad loved it here at this hotel so much, he bought a painting of it, set atop the cliff. It hung on the wall facing his bed. I asked him about it the week before he passed. He talked of the lovely wee beach of stones with a lift down onto it. He told us of the little hermitage/grotto he walked to and he sat and meditated in. He said we should go "some day". The painting was the last thing he was looking at when he passed, as we sat with him. So we came here.

We look out over the cliff to the sunrise over the sea and we look up at the stars at night before sleep. So you can imagine my surprise when I found this piece below, saved in the Notes App. It's an excerpt from a letter by Jill Kottmeier and you can find it at www.elephantjournal.com

"Speak my name often, tell my story, and teach everyone who comes into your path. Close your eyes and open your spirit and you will feel me beside you, guiding you every step of the way. You all gave me the best life a man could ask for."

Speechless again.

But as I post this Please Don't Stop The Music is playing for the Aqua Aerobics class I'm NOT in. And I hate Beyoncé but yesterday's Tune- In-My-Heid-All-Day, that I didn't figure out till later, was I Can See Your Halo.

# CHAPTER 11:
# APRIL 2017

SYNCHRONICITY

Yesterday I visited Schoenstatt, where my father went regularly to pray/meditate. I could almost feel him sitting next to me. My prayer was "I'm gonna put away your wee funeral card now Dad, I need to let you move on and I'll be okay." It sounded good, even if I didn't believe it myself.

I continued: "If there is any way you can give me a wee sign to let me know you're okay, I'd love that. A wee message that I'd understand. I miss you and I love you".

I sat. Nothing. Silence. A sunbeam ? Maybe that's it? I left.

My Dad loved all things angelic - I gave him a lovely figurine when he was diagnosed and she watched over him in his bed as he faded over the months.

I have a friend who took me along a couple of years ago to a psychic show. It's not something I DO, but she assured me this woman was "special" and had great integrity. She was also very funny and down to earth. Her name is Mary, Mary Angels. Yes, really.

I was very impressed with her accuracy and her modus operandus.

I got a message from a friend who had passed, that no-one else could have known. That was a couple of years ago. I haven't seen Mary since, she's a busy woman.

This morning Mary sent me a PM, completely out of the blue, explaining it's most unusual for her to do this.

She wrote: "Hello Angela, I hope u don't mind this wee message. It's not something I have a habit of doing. I was at Carfin grotto on

Monday trying to find some inner peace. As I walked away from the Angel Chapel, I connected to a man named Patrick. He said 'when the time is right for you Mary, can you tell Angela to let my family know I am truly at peace. He's glad u got your stuff you deserved'."

I thanked her profusely, explained a little of the significance, and she replied, "Aww Angela, I never ever send messages without the person's request, that's why I've sat on it since Monday. I am so glad I did and I really hope you get the love that was given to me to pass on. It's been a real tough time for you all, and all I can say is please believe your dad is very much around. Sending you the biggest hug I can send from cyber. Keep smiling. Xx"

Note: I got delivery a few weeks ago of some worthless, but priceless to me, items I had given my dad. And my dad's song was "When You're Smiling"

Grateful!

# CHAPTER 12:
# MAY 2017

GIFTS AND GRACE

Out walking this morning in glorious sunshine, I had time to reflect on a busy week of work in various forms, paid and unpaid: gardening, theraping, tutoring, managing, cooking, creating and admin-ing. It continues this weekend with teaching.

It dawned on me that somewhere along the line, the almost constant companion of emotional fog since my Father passed had cleared, and a deeper sense of connection and "feeling" had returned. I'm not sure exactly when or how, but it has.I was almost afraid to acknowledge it, lest just by thinking about it, it returned.

I realised that I've been living in a protective bubble; slightly distanced from life as I knew it B.D.I. - Before Dad's Illness.

This was a marvellous and ingenious survival system which buffered me from emotional overload, from "feeling too much".

It seems as if my soul is now saying it's time to take the training wheels off and start pedalling on your own. C'mon, you can do it.

People say time heals. I say it too. And it does. Of course it does.

But "The Missing" of those we have deeply loved? That, I think, only deepens over time. It occurred to me that, if I was sent away from my loved ones to prison for a year, or five years, that five years would be the tougher sentence. The longer the missing, the deeper the loss.

But I've noticed too that while at first I couldn't get past the memories of the illness, the dying, the funeral, the aftermath.. recently happier times from B.D.I. began to surface spontaneously. They percolate up for recognition now on an almost daily basis.

In therapy we call this "processing". We gradually recover from the traumatic memories, process them, and in time thereby gain access to more resourceful memories again.

With the recent beautiful sunshine came memories of laughing a lot in the garden with him, on holidays past and out walking - which we did a lot.

This last week or so I've experienced a lot of laughter, deep belly laughs returned replacing the Mona Lisa smile of recent months.

I've been deeply touched by the generosity of others - the £730 donated for last week's sponsored walk, the rose petal bath bomb from a student, the offer of a therapy bed electric blanket from a friend who is clearing out and thought of me, flowers and plants from house guests, colleagues going above and beyond to offer support at work. And finding the beautiful wee door at the garden centre for the fairy dell I'm creating just now.

This love and generosity is what sustains us. And we are called upon to receive them fully and experience gratitude but we need to remember to pay it forward too.

Somebody out there needs us today. How can we help? How can I be the reason somebody else experiences feeling loved, supported and has something to be grateful for today? Ask yourself that every day, and I will too.

THE HEALING POWER OF DREAMS
After four weary nights of sleeplessness, which I blamed on the Full Moon, Wagamama's monosodium glutomate, watching News at Ten, eating too late, pre-course teaching adrenaline and my hormones, I finally surrendered to a "reasonable night" of fair quality sleep last night.

And I got it. It's coming up to the six-month date of my Dad dying – Monday. Which, curiously, is also the anniversary of my pal Liz's death, 18 May.

Last night I had a beautiful dream of a vivacious yellow bird which came in my bedroom window and landed on my hand, before flying back out again.

A friend was also in the dream with his daughter at the age she would have been when he lost his wife many years ago. It felt like a really significant dream. I could still feel the featherlight touch of the beautiful bird on awakening.

I felt the message deeply - I wasn't alone. Good friends have fathers who are seriously ill; another has just lost her Mum; yet another's Mum has the same diagnosis as Dad; and another still is burying her sister-in-law shortly.

Death and loss touches us all. We are all going through this together, however long it's been, whatever the circumstances. We have ALL been touched, we all will be, again and again. I like to think that we are visited by our loved ones in our dreams and in our lives, if we are open to the signs and signals which bless us.

This morning while on my "wobbly machine" in the garage, my wee friend the robin appeared while I was listening to Caron Wheeler singing Don't Quit, which I rediscovered after a pal posted on FB this morning that the poem was found in her Mother's purse after her passing.

Today, after eating a ridiculous afternoon tea with my Mum at Duck Bay, I admired the plants I'd potted for her last week - they are all singing and dancing after the recent downpour. I "stole" some lavender, rosemary, sage and bought some roses to make a smudging stick to burn at my Reiki days as a symbol of cleansing and purification.

The symbolism wasn't lost on me. The cycle of life and growth, blooming and growing, surrender and loss, and transformation and blessing.

We are all in this cycle together... those we love, the birds, the flowers and all of us.

TRANSFORMATION

As my Dad placed the rock on the cairn in Sandeel's Bay, Iona, back in October 2015, he said: "This stone will be here for all time , even when we're not".

A part of me somehow KNEW what he was saying and sure enough, just over a year later, he wasn't "here". But it was so comforting to stand beside the Cairn last week on Iona - to have something "solid", something physical to touch, to remember. The song There's A Place For Us came to mind again.

His ashes will be scattered soon beside his parents' grave, plans are afoot. I know he is not there - of course I do - but I'm surprised at how comforted I feel to have a place to visit nearer home.

My heart melted again this week as I'm sure yours did, for the unnecessary and violent loss of such young lives in Manchester.

It's easy to get into the "Which Is Worse Grief Olympics" and somehow categorise and upgrade/downgrade loss and grief.

A tradesman helping us this week tried to downgrade his loss because his granny who had just died was 88. I watched him doing it, he couldn't understand why he was so shocked, so sore. He said, "After all, she was old and had a good life, not like the children at the Arena."

I've discovered a new and perverse guilt arising in me from time to time, when I hear about more recent losses and scary diagnoses from friends and colleagues. Yet another has been admitted to hospital with lung cancer. Guilt that I'm STILL hurting after all this time.

I nearly choked in a coffee shop last week on Iona to stop myself bursting into tears. It had begun as an angry ball in the pit of my stomach and it just grew and grew- until it was a dam-burst of unspent tears. Thankfully G spotted it, asked if I was okay and that alerted me and bought me time to run to the loo and sob in private for a while.

The place was chock-a-block and there was absolutely no trigger, nil, niente, nada. Just a downpour of grief, six months later!

And the sense that others are worse off can become a knotted rope to flay ourselves with....

Burns burn inwards. After a burn, you think you've held your finger under the tap long enough, because it's numb. But later, you realise it's still burning - inwards.

Grief burns inwards, if anything more viciously and for much longer. There is no time limit. The guilt and shame of burning deeper inside, long after the external formalities have passed and whilst others are fire-fighting their own blazes, needs to be handled with absolute gentleness and compassion.

Sometimes I can scare myself that if I don't "snap out of it", I'll become "addicted" to grief. I had an old great aunt who never recovered from her husband's death at an early age. I terrify myself that I'll end up like her - living in the past, stuck in history.

These are all the ways we can make ourselves wrong. Shame, fear, bullying, self-loathing, anger, frustration, hiding, numbing, anaesthetising, pretending, lying, distracting.

It's an uncharted sea of moving tides - that's grief. And I'm discovering depths of love, vulnerability and connection I may have missed out on had I gone first, before my loved ones.

There's a price for that. The pain and confusion are at times breathtaking. The sense of loneliness and isolation can be overwhelming. But we can do it, all of us.. because we are not alone.

When I stop comparing or competing in the Grief Olympics; when I put down the guilt & shame for STILL burning, and at times MORE than before; when I tear up contracts with deadlines for how I think I SHOULD be and stop judging myself in relation to others who are WORSE OFF... when I do all of that I soften, open and I can reach out my hand in mutual understanding to others walking on the Road Loss Travelled.

BALANCE

I was chatting with a friend yesterday whose Father is critically ill: she was describing how suddenly her life felt completely surreal as she engages in frontline combat with NHS budget constraints and staffing problems, both of which have directly led to delays and thereby severe complications, which have cost her Father dearly.

I could relate entirely and offered an analogy: "Do you feel like you're in a movie sometimes? Only nobody has sent you the script with your lines; and so you're improvising as you go?" She nodded.

For me, at these times, the movie runs in slow motion and is vaguely familiar at others, as if Im doing a retake of a scene I've done before.

I'm en route to London via Edinburgh to visit a very special friend I've known for over 30 years, who is terminally ill with lung cancer. He may be gone in a matter of weeks but a few months at best - it's Stage 4 and aggressive.

I am still in the bubble of shock, but I'm already grateful to have the opportunity to express my gratitude and appreciation for all he brought to my life; and to reminisce about the journey together over the years.

He, like dad, is very brave ("I'm not afraid") and philosophical about all of it. He even shared some worldly wisdom on the phone as a "parting gift".

Though we've not spent a lot of time together in recent years, partly due to geography, I will still miss him greatly. He played a huge part in my life and was a great support, especially in my younger years, when he was almost a surrogate father figure.

He's going to start taking Cannabis Oil, which has been receiving some interesting feedback in relation to a number of medical conditions, including chronic pain, IBS, MS and cancer itself and which is now, just recently, legal to buy in the UK. Though a reputable supplier of high grade and correct percentage level of purity for requirements is advised, along with the correct type & dosage advice. They are NOT all the same; just like most things you can source online. I was glad that I was able to direct him to a naturopathic practitioner who dispenses it, and I'm delivering it to him while I'm down.

It was great to hear that his doctors are totally supportive of his decision to start it. They have nothing they can offer him; no chemo/no surgery, only pain relief. And the oil allegedly offers pain relief too.

It's all surreal - 30 years later, on the train to Central London, where it all began, to visit him - this time though it's ME who has something to offer him.

SENDING A SIGN

Tavistock Square, where Gandhi overlooks the site of the 7/11

Bus Bomb, a mere 20 yards away. A place of amazing tranquility and beauty, to focus and to draw breath, as a wee squirrel joined us and drank from a puddle.

A friend responded to my post from yesterday, this morning and recommended a book, When Breath Becomes Air by Paul Kalanithi. Here is my reply. Thanks so much Cherie, an amazing book, I discovered as it winked at me in a bookshop in Aberfeldy, shortly after my dad died last year.

I was desperate for a "sign" or a "message" that he was okay on the other side of the veil. It fell open at this section, near the end, when he is writing a message to his baby daughter.

"You filled a dying man's days with a sated joy, a joy unknown to me in all my prior years, a joy that does not hunger for more and more but rests, satisfied. In this time, right now, that is an enormous thing."

I can't tell you, how much that comforted me Cherie, and how much your message did the same as it reminded me of that experience.

Coincidence? I'd like to think not. Thank you.

PS I Googled the book this morning and found the quote in a review. Huge comfort. Read it!

# CHAPTER 13:
# JUNE 2017

A TALE OF THREE ROSES

My Father's ashes are being scattered on Tuesday. At last - it's been a long wait. I received the news of the death of a mentor, friend and colleague who died Tuesday this week. I've known him 32 years and he was a father figure to me.

Another friend's Dad died on Monday, although I'd never met him, my heart was sore for her. Today's weather matched my mood when I awoke....cloudy, dreich, gusty and unpredictable, with a chill and gloom.

But I have a Reiki 2 this weekend to teach, so an early rise was needed to prepare the house for my students tomorrow. The garden needed a check, tweak and tidy too and we've spent quite a bit of time on it lately. So I'm pretty aware of what's growing where.

The rose: a white one from me ; a yellow one from my Mother (Symbol of Eternal Love), these I placed on the coffin at the funeral of my Father.

You can imagine my surprise, then, when I looked out the window after arising this morning in my grumpy whinging state, to see something I've never noticed growing in the middle of our hedge. Only a single white rose. Gotcha!

"All will be well, and all manner of things shall be well," Julian of Norwich.

THE VEIL IS THIN

"24 hours, two butterflies, three feathers and two Dads being laid to rest with an hour of each other".

Coincidences! Don't you just love them, but call them something else?

So, yesterday I'm chatting to G outside and notice a pure white curly feather at my feet. I pick it up, put in my pocket, then G says "it's landed in your hair, it must've flown out!"

I try to retrieve it, it blows down the path. I chase it but it blows through the shut gate and I'm losing it to the breeze. I jokingly say "come back!"... and it blows back to my feet.

Last night I find yet another identical feather at my feet in the bedroom, by the dressing table.

Today I'm chatting on phone to Sharon at the Clinic, who mentions an event at St. Mary's church near the Harvest. I say, "Oh, there's that name again (St.Mary's, Edinburgh, and another St Mary's in the East End of Glasgow were where my dad's journey began and ended), and we are scattering Dad's ashes tomorrow at his parents' grave.

I look down to the ground, and yes, it's identical feather number three.

Last night I was driving two pals a 40-minute journey to another friend's for dinner. As we parked, Irene said: "OMG! There's been a red admiral butterfly inside the car the whole way here, it just flew out as I opened the door!".

This morning, I have a quick cuppa with G outside. I'm telling him about last night, and another red admiral only lands on the plant right beside him and sits for ages.

My friend's Dad is being cremated at 10 tomorrow; we are scattering my dad's ashes an hour later.

The veil can be as thin as you perceive it to be, when you watch for the signs and signals along the way.

CLOSURE

I "walked in my Father's moccasins" this morning, as I got ready to say a final goodbye, by burying his ashes beside his parents.

Although I hated the delays, in hindsight it has taken THIS long to move through the shock, denial, confusion and emotional upheaval all round. So I felt much more "present" than I did at the funeral seven months ago, but this was a double-edged sword: I was much more RAW. This was for real, this time, not anaesthetised by the mental Valium of shock. I felt every word, heard every sound and I knew this was for real; no doubt about it. God bless you Caroline Miller for your homeopathic Ignatia, I had some left and, oh my, it helped a lot.

We were four minutes late but called ahead to advise. We were stuck behind not one, but two different bin lorries, on two different sections, doing 22mph on the rain-washed roads. Then the Sat-Nav Twit tried to direct us to The Necropolis in Glasgow, and not The Western Necropolis we had fed in, a five mile round-trip. The mantras/expletives were choice, I can tell you.

I was stuck behind the old rubbish which needed dumped. And I was temporarily being taken in the wrong direction until I followed my gut, veered onto my own intuitive path, and arrived slightly later than planned. But I arrived.

What a metaphor. It was suitably dreich, the sky cried tears to blend with mine. It wasn't surreal this time.

G pointed out the ceramic robin on the gravestone of Dad's neighbour. What joy. I took it as a sign of permission to "borrow" one of his neighbours' 12 WHITE, yes I did say WHITE roses, and place it in with his casket of ashes. I will replace it with a whole bunch on my next visit.

My G & I cried with the rain in the car afterwards. It was a tough morning.

But we regrouped. Will Fyffe, the Glasgow Poet, is buried a few metres away and his plaque reads "I belong to Glasgow". This made us smile.

A comforting cappuccino at Dobbies soothed our hearts followed by a Eusibi's Real Italiano Pinsa and shared heart-attack-on-a-plate-home-made-doughnut. I told myself it was covered in Angel-dust.

I'm now enjoying a wee glass of Malbec, and toasting my Captain, and the man by my side, my Lord of the Grey Home, who held me up today.

Here's to the men who are heroes for all the right reasons. Don't worry- he's got my back - sleep tight dad.

LIFE GOES ON.

Someone wrote a beautiful message to me today , which expressed her gratitude for my posts on living, loving, and grieving. I have been regularly asking myself when to "give it a rest" and move on to a cheerier theme of writing. Maybe I'm becoming a "damper", reminding people of what they've gone through, are going through or have still to go through.

Should I put my Father to bed and move on now that his ashes are scattered?

I think my question was answered by two teachers of mine in their recent writings, which I read this morning. Richard Rohr was reflecting on the direct relationship between my compassion and empathy levels for the brokenness and absurd confusion of things in our world and the people in it; and my compassion and empathy for the brokenness and confusion which lives inside of me; inside of all of us, for that matter.

He writes about how when we judge or criticise "the poor" and particularly people on benefits, we should remember that "we are ALL on benefits". We all live on the mercy of the Divine, the Universe, God, Gaia, whatever term floats yer boat. We would do well to remember that. I'm living on handouts and sometimes emergency relief from the Great Mystery every day.

When I stay connected, from a loving place, to all that is broken and hurting "out there", I am also staying connected to what is to be healed "in here" and vice-versa. Richard recommends a balance of both contemplation and action, inside of ourselves and outside in the world. But cautions that we need BOTH to be wholly (Holy) effective.

I realised that this is my motivation for continuing to share my own experiences of living, loving, grieving and healing. I WILL pull the book together of my contemplations over this past year and donate all profits to pancreatic cancer. A former student came out of the blue to offer to help pull it together.

My other Spiritual Teacher, Jim Finley, gave me some guidance through a friend in the States who shared from a talk she attended of his recently.

He said "I will keep touching the Hurting Place with love. And at the end of my life, all that will be left is love. And then I will truly be God's presence in the world"

# CHAPTER 14:
# JULY 2017

MOVES AND MENTORS

Driving and sailing solo on the Waves Less Travelled, in very low cloud on Mull, en route to The Thin Place of Iona.

My friend Sister Jean is leaving here next week after 15 years: she is a Heart Mother to me; but she's moving closer.. to Dalkeith.

It will, however, change everything for her and for us when we visit here.

This has been a time of many endings recently.

My colleague and principal of the London College I teach for, Michael Joseph, is being cremated in Southern England on Tuesday. Over 30 years of working together. I was so glad I visited him in hospital a few weeks ago in London. The trip down again would take another two full days of travel, so I'm saying goodbye from here on Iona, in spirit, on Tuesday morning at 9.30am.

Endings are a part of the circle of life and they are painful, if we try to hold on too much, too hard, too long.

While you can't "speed up" or fake letting go, you can be mindful of where, when and how you are gripping, or clinging on for dear life; living in a state of not very well-hidden yet quiet desperation. We can notice what is keeping us "stuck" and not serving us; and other times when we simply need-to-be-stuck in order to keep breathing.

One of my mentors used to say "Learn to be a good loser, We are going to do a lot of it in our lifetime; and the sooner you learn/practice the art of losing, the easier your life will become".

The guy who helps with our garden Tony, just buried his gran one week, then the following week, had his garden shed burgled by a nutter - with a machete, who he had to flee and lock all doors, as said burglar tried to kick his way into the house.

The couple switching off life-support for their beloved child Charlie.

A dear friend, Irene, watching her dad undergo radiotherapy to stop his internal bleeding, after months of illness and worry.

My pal Lorna who buried her dad on Tuesday.

The people of Iona grieving the departure of one of the most beautiful souls to grace the community here on the Island, Sister Jean.

Sister Jean at nearly 80 years old adjusting to a new role and environment as director of a care home for elderly sisters in a busy town; away from the peace & calm of her island home of 15 years.

And me! Still raw and sore after scattering my Dad's ashes this week, and losing another huge influence and important man, Michael, who was a distant father-figure in my life.

Loss, letting go, how can we help ourselves though it? I asked how Jean managed to be so cheery when she is leaving in a week, for good.

She said she had "done the work" and come through the other side. For sure, she has felt the feelings big time for weeks and months. She didn't fly through with her halo polished. She had to contend with the anger, fear, bargaining, denial, shock, anxiety and regret; sat, walked and cried, and worked through the feelings with good, solid support; but then moved on into acceptance. Although the less "spiritually evolved" among us - like ME - usually circle back around the old wagons several times for good measure.

And then came the gratitude for all she'd been given; the anticipation and excitement about new beginnings and opportunities; horizons not yet seen. She will miss the place and people, that's for sure; there will be challenges during the transition; but she has high hopes for new wonderful, interesting and fulfilling experiences. She will continue to serve, wherever she lays her hat.. that's where she'll make her home.

I thought of my journey up here through the tears and rain, the mist and cloud. Through all the wild and at times thundery, stormy weather and rough terrain... ALL OF IT WAS BREATHTAK-ING, scary at times, but spectacular and awe-inspiring. Mean and moody in places but always alive and changing by the second. Every single step of the way. And now I'm here in my temporary spiritual grace-filled home, for now. Until I move on again. Oh yeah, and the road trip up was kinda similar too.

# CHAPTER 15:
# AUGUST 2017

ON SILK PURSES AND SOW'S EARS

I'm en route to Iona to deliver my annual retreat next weekend to a group and decided to break the journey in Oban, so booked into an economical hotel, if a tad shabby-chic. Recent distracting events meant I was behind on preparation, so I decided to finish off the course content over the two days I would have on Iona to set up and prepare before the group arrive. I'm travelling solo for this one, as Lord G is holding the fort and babysitting Sir Ian (the cat).

I fell into bed around midnight, after an adrenaline-filled journey in torrential rain through puddles like lakes, and a constant waterfall over my windscreen.

For some reason unbeknown to me I put my suitcase up against the door. At 2.22am, I awoke to the cacophony of two men's voices outside my door, followed by a key in the lock, the door opening, the suitcase falling over and the silhouette of two burly men in my room.

I yelled "Get out, get out!" and after a minute of confusion, they backed out, muttering between them. I bolted out of bed and snibbed the door.

I was in shock, but regained the presence of mind to phone reception. I blurted out the story to be told the Duty Manager had come to the wrong floor to let a guy in with the master key, as he had lost his.

I gave him a short tutorial in the depth of my feelings about the matter.

Of course, sleep escaped me for the rest of the night: my adrenaline was having a party now - so a herbal tea was in order.

To distract my mind, I played on my phone . The first post I read led me on to a comment below it: a heart-melting piece of poetry about life which had tremendous depth and meaning for me, beautifully crafted and "other-worldly". It was signed off simply by the poet's first name: PATRIC . Which, of course, was my dear Captain's name.

I was on a roll. Then I discovered two perfect quotes; a song by Ed Sheeran I'd never heard before - perfect for the retreat; and an amazing YouTube video with the information I'd been looking for to plug a gap in my course content.

I cooried in and scribbled in the dark, as the dawn blinked its way through the curtains and the sounds of the fishermen's boats began to leave the harbour. By 5.30am the material was complete. Voila!

Love moves in mysterious ways.

I was up, showered and dressed by 6.30am and yes, it will be a nap and an early tonight after two hours of sleep. And yes, of course, I asked for a refund, which I received with a full and heartfelt apology.

ON THE SHOWER-SOUND-BATHING TECHNIQUE FOR GRIEF.
Absolutely Free Masterclass

We all feel like shit sometimes. The after-effect of Monday's fuller-than-Full-Moon left me dazed and punch-drunk after a 12-hour journey back from Iona on Tuesday. We worked hard on Iona, as always, and the magnetic "poultice effect" of the island had done the trick. I returned feeling much more open and vulnerable than the slightly calcified tin-woman who had driven up the week before, with all her defences in military alignment.?

However, we need some de-compression time when we are resurfacing or changing altitude - and this week there wasn't much. It was straight back in.

On arising in the morning, I was blindsided and under a severe and persistent sniper attack of grief and loss on Wednesday and

Thursday, which completely ambushed me. I miss my Dad. I miss so much. I miss the things that should have happened afterwards, but didn't. It has been a really hard and hellish journey back from his death, for so many reasons. But they are not for here.

It arose from a new hiding place - deep down and at the back of my belly - causing gasping, shaky and wobbly sobs which were "new", curious and strangely comforting. I felt like a blancmange .

So I went out for a walk, with hankie-lined pockets, and tried to outrun the invading forces. To no avail. The assault was relentless. The sheep and coos in the fields observed me with a startled bemusement. They too were surprised at this public oversharing of emotion.

What to do? Take the whole.bottle of Kalms in the medicine cupboard, cancel work, turn up at A&E with "canny-stop-crying-itis" or pray for help?

I did the last one, I prayed.

I found myself making my way purposefully back home, locating the boom-box speaker for my iPhone. I turned on the shower to the "gloriously hot" setting, I locked the door. I selected the saddest, weepiest, toe-curlingly painful, victim-iest, most abandoned songs I could find - e.g. Bonnie Raitt, Kate Bush, Todd Rundgren, Beth Nielsen Chapman, Ed Sheeran - turned up the volume and began my Shower-Soundbath-Therapy

This is where you just melt into the shower and become one enormous stream of tears. You BECOME the tears, hold nothing back, make as much noise as you want - because the music is BLARING and nobody could hear you anyway. And you sing as many lyrics as you can remember and make up the rest.

For as long as you have or need, you "squeeze the juice" out of every sad lyric until you have either run out of tears or turned into a prune.

When you are All Cried Out (as Alison Moyet sang), you then switch on a contrasting dancing/happy/powerful/upbeat song and dance wildly, untamed and naked still under the shower. Finishing with a big shaggy dog shake to dry off . "Let The River Run" by Carly Simon, "Rhythm of Life" by Sammy Davis Jnr. And

"Happy" by Pharrell Williams lit my fire.

I've tried this three mornings in a row now and it works a treat.

"GREET ON DEMAND!" The episodes are shorter each time.

I'm not planning to run any workshops on this technique yet, until I've embarked on a diet and exercise regime followed by a short course of Liposuction and bum-lift. After that I hope to upload some short demo videos on YouTube to promote, and release the book with photo illustrations to guide the practice. I may wear a bodysuit.

Feel free to try it out yourself, FB hearties.. it's good to share!

DAD'S LOST HAT

I've had a couple of days of mostly bedrest, with only a few hours of upright activity thrown in. I've been pole-axed by a lurgy, and thankfully had diary space to allow myself horizontal quiet time. This birthed some deep thinking on my recent inner sadness.

I heard it said when your HEART is broken into pieces - you should make ART from those pieces. So I'm doing just that - writing and soon to be painting. Writing, and expressing my feelings, has been my saving grace.

I recently discovered that I've lost my Dad's hat. The discovery surprised me, in that I was not devastated. I was surprised how okay I was about it. I've never been great with hats, gloves or sunglasses, always losing accessories. So it was pretty inevitable I suppose.

I realised that I have simply become so desensitised to loss generally over the past eight months, there's been so much of it, that having a meltdown over a hat seemed daft. I've got a photo of it.

Losing my Dad was the hardest thing so far; but losing my faith in others I had loved and trusted who were still alive, that was a close second.

It's been quite a time of reflection. I didn't just lose a Father or a hat; I lost much, much more. But the pain of the loss of the "externals" pushed me deeper and deeper inside to discover a new world of art, music, writing, photography - my inner landscape which is ever -expanding. The assholes did me a favour!

And it's time to release them to the past - where they belong. To move on; to cut the cords that bind.

"There is still a beauty in grief. Your grief shows that you have risked opening up your life and your heart to someone". John O' Donoghue

## THE HAT RETURNS!

So I'd lost the hat - the one Dad wore when we went to Iona together - and I had "borrowed" when he was ill. I'd cleared out the shelf for hats and scarves three times, desperately looking, before this year's Iona visit. It was gone.

Last week, after a deep chat on the phone with a family member about him, I went to the same shelf to find a scarf.. and his hat fell out and landed at my feet. Even G was shocked, he knew how much I'd hunted for it, and how sad I had been from losing it.

It's been the trickiest of times lately - every sector of life has had its challenges; not one area has been on solid ground . The shifting has been palpable and I don't remember feeling so over-stretched, though Im sure I have been.

I hadn't felt the connection to my Father's presence for a while but I had a "chat" with him anyway. It felt pretty one-way.

I was curious then this week, when the same family member, from the phone call prior to the curious-case-of-the-missing-hat, confided that they had awoken during the early hours of Monday to the sense of my dad "kneeling beside the bed", watching over them, as if in prayer. This is NOT this person's normal chat, nor comfort zone. It wasn't a flesh and bone experience, but they swore they KNEW it was him.

# CHAPTER 16:
# SEPTEMBER 2017

ON WHAT FLOATS YOUR BOAT?

Do YOU know?

Julie Andrews knew. "Raindrops on roses, and whiskers on kittens, bright copper kettles and warm woolen mittens..."

Sometimes we find ourselves beached, blown by the storms of life up on to the shore. And we need to take refuge there for a while, until the storm blows itself out.

But too often, we remain there - afraid or unsure of how to put out to sea and feel the wind in our sails, carrying us forward to new horizons.

I certainly experienced quite a lot of "all washed up" and grounded times after the death of my father nine months ago. And my job as a therapist is to support others who are washed ashore; stuck and unable to travel on.

How do you refloat a boat?

We need help, support, assistance, more power. We simply can't do it alone by brute force; we are left exhausted and frustrated. We have to ask for help - reach out to others to get back in the water. We need to risk getting wet, jump in, grab the oars and start rowing; get the sails up, find the direction of the wind and have a compass to direct us. Otherwise we may find ourselves going backwards or end up grounded ashore again.

Asking for help is tricky, because we have to make ourselves vulnerable when we admit we need help. And let's be honest, some folks WILL see it as a weakness and try to take advantage. That's why we don't want to do it! But when we ask, we will always find some souls, eventually, who will come to our aid and help us carry and push our boat back out to sea. Not all, but some. And that's enough - all we need, in fact.

If you are feeling "beached" just now, ask yourself 'who can help me put out to sea?'. Ask for support/assistance from those people. Are YOU helping you? Or are you sitting on the shoreline with your head in your hands

Do you have a compass and a map (sense of direction, even if it's only to get off this dang beach); sustenance and fuel for the journey (good nutrition, air, rest/sleep, inspired reading, body movement)?

Are you ready to wait for the wave to carry you, take hold of the oars and row; put your sails up again and let the winds of life and love carry you on to new places, new people, new experiences?

Who do you want to take on the boat with you? Who do you need to leave behind? Bless them standing on the shoreline with a goodbye wave.

We need to reflect on, and know, what floats our boat, what and who sustains us, where we are and where we want to go;or we can find ourselves all washed up, stuck and grounded while our precious life is passing us by.

ON NOT SO ABSENT FRIENDS

Yesterday G and I sloped off early for a quiet breakfast a deux and to visit the Church of the Angels in Pollensa. For such a small town they have a massive convent and three or four large churches. Even the Patisserie names a cake in honour of the angels.

It is a very peaceful place to sit inside the coolness and stillness of the church, with its heavenly stained glass window.

I prayed for all I remembered and included my Dad, who loved all things angel-related. My last thought was, "I've been pretty busy and distracted, Dad, but here I am so I'm sure if you were gonna get my attention with a wee sign, now would be the time and place".

Nothing. Not even a sunbeam or an extra flickery candle flame.

G motioned with a nod and the hand signal for coffee time, so I got up to leave.

As soon as I walked out of the church and turned my head, I guffawed at the the signage of the shop in the adjacent lane: DA-DA!

Apart from the obvious Glaswegian reference to the title of father, my Dad used to arrive at family events, with a flourish, and declare "Da-Da!", as in an orchestral salute for a performer's arrival on stage. We both clocked it, then G pointed to the sign on the next shop along the lane: "Welcome to Peace of Mind - protecting what you care most about". Incredible. He had me at "Da-Da".

These wee synchronicities are bittersweet, comforting but opening. That's the thing about holidays - they slow us down and the protective and defended layers melt. I was grateful for my sunglasses as tears of "The Missing" freely flowed and memories of holidays past, with Pat present, surfaced.

But I did find La Shoppe with the perfect dress and the even more perfect ear-rings: spiral circles. The circle of life; just like the spiral of candles in which I had placed mine in the church, the spiral angel cake and the stained glass window.

Thanks Dad and if yours, like mine, has passed over the Veil, send up a wee prayer today. If you still have yours here then give them a call/visit/hug and tell them you love them in whatever way feels right. You are blessed.

# CHAPTER 17: NOVEMBER 2017

**SOMETHING STUPID**

Met Mum for lunch – Dad's first anniversary is looming.

As we drove down to the restaurant, we stopped at traffic lights; I've just noticed a cafe there is called P.J.'s

His initials were Patrick Joseph and his nickname was PJ.

Strike two came as I drove off, an oncoming car had the registration plate "PAT 26".

Strike three landed 30 minutes later in the restaurant when Frank and Nancy sang "Something Stupid" - our party piece together. For his 80th we recorded it on CD with a mobile studio I hired as his pressie. I call that a triple whammy, in jig time.

**A CLOUD OF LOVE**

Thank you for your heartfelt messages today; I felt surrounded in a cloud of love. Lord G and I went to the Carmelite Convent again, to where Dad joined us on many a meditation day. We listened to "the angels singing", even though the average age is about 70.

Visiting the graveside was tough - his name is now engraved on the headstone, so stark a reminder. I reread all the beautiful cards from a year ago and I will burn them tonight in the fire - another letting-go.

At Dobbies for coffee, G bought me a holly tree to plant in Dad's memory in the garden and we passed a Punch and Judy show. It brought back many wonderful childhood memories, like the carousel horses memories of Butlin's as a child: "the painted ponies go up and down". The two angels and bunny hanging over Punch's tent didn't go un-noticed either!

My silent but strong soulmate, G, carried me through a tough day. He is grieving too but always on duty. 5.50 pm was the time of passing over; we will sit quiet with Shirley's beautiful candle then. Feel free to join in for all the souls we love and miss.

## ONE YEAR TODAY

I had thought of lots of "clever things" to write today, but as I awoke this morning , to beautiful sunshine , the word inside my heart was simply GRATEFUL.

Thank you Dad, for giving me life; being a life -saver; being a life-giver; a lover of life and one of my Soulfriends, an Anam Cara.

You taught me to Sing in the Rain, Smile Though My Heart Was Aching, Walk On The Sunny Side of The Street and that When You're Smiling The Whole World Smiles With You.

Forgive me if today I canny quite manage that: I miss you too much. x

Rest in Peace Pat Trainer (11.4.35-18.11.16)

## ON EVEN MORE SYNCHRONICITY

My Father's first anniversary was on Saturday. After visiting the grave, which was a tough call as it was the first time I had seen his name on the headstone, we called in for a cuppa to Kim's.

When I was a wee girl, apparently I used to ask why I was called Angela and my Dad would say, "because you are an angel".

I responded, "But I'm NOT an angel!".

This, it seems, was a regular game.

So, it was with some surprise that when we arrived, Miss Ella went off to change into one of her many costumes and unknowing of the above history, made her entrance resplendent in halo, wand and wings! As I announced "look it's an angel!", she replied, "I'm NOT an angel!".

On the headstone on Sunday I noticed the carving of praying hands. As I left, I pressed my hand over them, to say goodbye.

So it was with some surprise that when we arrived on Sunday on our wee break in the sun, (G's birthday pressie) the wall art in the bedroom was a painting of two hands. Granted, not praying, but beautifully henna-ed.

Out walking on Tuesday, I was thinking of my Dad a lot - he loved walking by the sea - and chatting intermittently about him to G. I'm sure I wrote last year about how apt it was that the last sound he made, as he passed over the Veil, was a hearty "HA!" - which was so apt for him. He laughed a lot! Imagine our surprise when we walked past a huge boulder on the beach promenade, with "HA" written in 12-inch letters; nothing else.

Setting off today for more adventures, living closer to the thin place that quietness and silence welcomes in.

ON CLOSING A CHAPTER

When I started to post about my father's terminal illness last year, I had no idea that so many people would respond to my posts with their own insights and speak about their journeys with their loved ones. So I kept on writing.

The responses grew and continued through his subsequent passing and I carried on sharing about my journey through the grieving process.

For me it was very therapeutic and the loving words of support and sharing of others was incredibly healing. It was never easy and often cost me emotionally. I knew there was also a groundswell of disapproval lurking in the background; I could almost hear the "tut-tuts" in the distance and received my fair share of negative feedback/dismay from some quarters. I lost some folk along the way.

But I wouldn't/couldn't stop. I felt as if I had something to say that perhaps others couldn't and that I had a job to do which made some sense of the pain and confusion.

A year on now from the funeral, I feel it's time to stop. I will collate my postings into a little booklet and self-publish to share with anyone who feels it may be beneficial to them or others.

I hope to start that process in the New Year. I will donate proceeds to Pancreatic Cancer Research in memory of my dad.

I would like to thank everyone who responded, shared, liked -

your support was priceless on this journey. And even those who disapproved or were horrified by such a public display of grief - you were also my teachers. I learned as much about the different effects of grief and grieving, and how we all handle things in our own way.

To quote Fritz Perles: "You do your thing; I do my thing. If we meet along the way, that's beautiful. If not, it can't be helped".

Of course, I won't NOT ever refer to my dad on Facebook again - that would be too sad; but I will find new subjects to write about and privately journal my continuing journey with the loss of my dad.

It's just time now.

# CHAPTER 18:
# DECEMBER 2017

NOT THE NEW YEAR RESOLUTION SHOW! from Sunny Aberfeldy.

"It was the worst of times; it was the best of times."

As I prepare to leave 2017 behind, I breathe a sigh of release. It was arguably one of the most difficult and painful years I have lived so far. At times it felt like I had changed channels on my lifescreen and many of the characters in my storyline suddenly donned pantomime costumes and masks, revealing familiar characters from childhood fables.

It was a surreal journey through the spooky forest with wicked witches, ugly sisters, wolves in sheep's clothing, poisoned apples, thorned roses, naked kings on horseback, cackling crones, curses and spells and all the usual themes you'd expect.

It was also a year of being cracked open, like a grain of wheat, spilling out everything contained inside to be transformed by life. Out poured everything I'd ever learned up until this time, to prepare me for my journey through the wild and unfamiliar territory.

I had to do it alone; these hero's/orphan's journeys don't have room for passengers, but I've had a great supporting cast. The ones who know me never once doubted me, and had my back at all times.

Yesterday in a cafe, the soundtrack of old songs playing was all my dad's stuff. "Bewitched, Bothered and Bewildered" was one; "Could It Be Magic"; "And I Love You So", finishing with "The Circle of Life" from the Lion King.

Promptly followed by an ad for "Singin' in the Rain"! The irony of the lyrics was not lost on me.

Today, for me, is about collecting acorns, just like the squirrels - sustenance for the Winter's journey.

There's plenty of time for planting new seeds in the Spring.

What did I learn this year; what did life teach me; what were the lessons?

Where did I let myself down? To whom and how can I make amends for my part in it all, where I've let myself down?

What were the fruits and gifts of this year 2017's harvest? What will sustain me on the journey over the pause/threshold into the New Year with the secret promises it holds?

This time is a time of punctuation which allows us to take stock, reflect and be transformed by it, if we do the work.

Now, I recommend a gratitude letter to God/Maya/Gaia/Allah/ The Universe/ Love/The Mysterons.

Earth School is a pretty amazing place, if at times rather scary and lonely, to learn how to polish your soul up like a diamond. But it can sometimes be quite dirty work. So take a soft cloth and, after rinsing off the debris, buff up your diamond to see just how much progress you've made this past year.?

I recommend long warm bath in Epsom, Himalayan or Dead Sea Salts in candlelight before the year turns, allowing the salts to draw out all toxic waste/psychic wounds symbolically. And following by smoothing on some lovely lotions or oils representing the gratitudes for the year, the people/places/animals/knowledge/books/blessings and gifts abundantly received.

I wish you all a blessed and healthy, vibrant, abundant and REAL guid New Year.

When you have procrastinated on pulling together the FB posts you wrote over a year or so ago, about your father's conscious living and conscious dying - whether through busyness, lack of technical expertise and/or abject fear of ridicule and a pal - Monica Smith - says tonight: "It's okay - I've checked - your posts are all still on Facebook. I will copy and paste them all into a Word Document, in date order and forward to you so you can organise

printing into a book". What can you say but "Thank You"?
After a wee greet of course.

# CHAPTER 19: FEBRUARY 2018

ON FRIENDSHIP

On the same day that a friend/confidante that I haven't seen for over a year sent a lovely wee gift from a recent visit to Saint Patrick's Cathedral in Dublin - in honour of my Dad Patrick (who passed 15 months ago), another friend and colleague asked me to help her with an article she is writing on friendship and give her some quotes.

She's asked me some soul-searching questions: many I feel ill-equipped to answer.

But the value I place on my long-standing palships (some are nearly 50 years in the can), work-related friendships and, more recent "freshly-baked" friendships is immense. Yet they are all so very different.

But on reflecting on my answers to Monica for her article I realised they all have one thing in common. They all require SACRIFICE.

That manifests in many forms: effort, tolerance, stamina, compromise, appreciating differences, forgiveness, lowering expectations and on and on.. and that's just what THEY need to sacrifice to put up with ME.

But, of course, I jest: it goes two ways. Both parties have to be willing to pay the price to enjoy the fruits that a healthy friendship provides. And that means that they need to be willing to tread water at times, endure jaggy moments, hold tongues, count to 20, risk honesty, risk rejection and hold the tension that true intimacy brings.

I felt a deep gratitude at my friend's act of generous thoughtfulness , after a year where I haven't fulfilled promises to meet up, since I last saw her at my Father's funeral. I was busy - distracted - away - Christmas - projects - drama-dealing - unwell: life rolled on and over a year had passed by. But her unconditional friendship held the space for me throughout all of that time. And so, she thought of me and bought and sent the gift. She was willing to pay the price with no guarantee of return on her investment.

True and deep friendship is certainly not for the faint-hearted, and not a journey of self-gratification. It is not a fuzzy warm feeling between two people.

True and deep friendship is a decision; it's an action; it's a VERB. To "friend" is to risk, share, endure, support, to receive and sometimes to hurt/be hurt.

It is an investment - and it costs us to invest.

Are YOU willing to pay the price? I am.

## THE POWER OF STOP

When G reminded me he had three nights offski in Bilbao, Spain for father and son time (David's 60th birthday gift ), I thought "Great! Catch-up time!".

I had a wee list of folks I owed dinner to, had rainchecked coffee with, my turn for a sleepover, could offer a lift for hospital visits to, haven't visited for ages, etc etc. Soon my weekend began to resemble my clinic diary.

Time for travel needed to be factored in; shopping for guests; bed-making, and soon my brain began to feel as if I wanted to run it under a tap.

I listened to its groans and moans.

I stopped. Here was a wonderful window of opportunity for a STOP THE WORLD WEEKEND and I was just about to miss it.

I tore up my dance card and left the whole darn three days blank. Yes, I said BLANK.

Unplanned spontaneity is a precious and rare gift for many of us, but often the habit of scheduling and busy life, commitments and obligations bleeds into the gaps - whether of minutes, hours or days.

And we fill them up ahead of time. Not allowing ourselves to risk feeling the space, the "abyss" of doing nothing, with nothing to do but wait and see how we feel.

So, nothing and nobody is having a piece of me ahead of time. I have resisted invitations, heavy hints of need and thinly veiled disapproval (or was it envy?).

The only name written into the diary for this weekend, across all three days, is "ANGELA". It's her weekend.

I may sleep indefinitely, have a midnight candle bath, watch all 43 seasons of Outlander, invent a new recipe, stare at the wild geese in the field opposite, play the piano and sing for my Dad over the Veil and Ian the Cat, write my journal at 3am and wait for the sunrise.

I may go pray to a wee favourite chapel in the Campsies, read a whole book from cover to cover, walk from the marina along the Canal, but I will wait to see what way the wind blows. I may do none of the above.

My new working title of my book-ette could be "EAT-PRAY-SLEEP-STOP!"

We sometimes, in our busy lives, lose the art of waiting for the wave and allowing ourselves to float and be carried. It's a reminder of what is actually happening anyway, when all's said and done.

ON SACRED TEARS

Maybe it was the glorious sight of the hundreds of wild geese last night on my way home, reminding me of the massive flock I watched passing over his home a day or two before my dad passed.

Maybe it was the unusual dream I had last night with two of his old pals in it.

Maybe it was the effect of giving myself a few days of peace and quiet while G is offski cycling around Bilbao and road testing the Rioja vineyards, though hopefully not at the same time!

Maybe it was the pull of the oncoming full moon, drawing emotions to the surface like a poultice.

Maybes aye, maybes naw.

But this morning, a familiar restlessness surfaced which no amount of bed-changing, furniture re-arranging nor laundry sorting would appease.

A wave of deep grief knocked me sideways and, in amongst the tangle of bed linen, clean and not yet clean, I surrendered to the pull of the tide.

I lost time. Real emotional release is usually timeless. But I remembered to breathe. That's pretty important. These layers of grief and repressed emotions need air and space to surface. They need time and space too.

Mondays were often "our day" - my dad and I met pretty regularly for lunch when he wasn't off globe-trotting. But unconsciously I have, with hindsight, managed to keep my Mondays pretty full and busy of late. I hadn't realised this until now.

I just miss him. I miss the belly-laughs; the trivial chatter; the banter; the deep philosophical discourses on spirituality; the daft songs; dafter antics; his ability to turn memories of his childhood into technicolour movie extravaganzas; regale us with detailed musings of our shared past, and of life B.A. (Before Angela).

I miss him.

A friend said recently that she thought the second year of grieving her mum was harder than the first. I don't agree. I think it's just "different" - not harder, not easier, just different.

It is perhaps a more hidden, secretive and reclusive form of grief. Only those "IN THE CLUB" truly recognise it - those who have been through it already themselves.

Perhaps it is the expectation and pressure we put on ourselves, in our Fast-Fix, Self-Help; three minutes to heal yer life culture that makes it harder to understand.

Grief is a slow-cooker. It percolates, it simmers and comes to boil most unexpectedly. It can be a great teacher, if we allow it, and don't succumb to anaesthetising ourselves or denying its expression.

Tears are a pure gift. They cleanse the soul. They soften the heart.

They bless us.

So, even though I used the wrong sheets (the freshly-laundered clean ones!) to dry my leftover mascaraed eyes and blow my nose, leaving a "Holy Shroud" on them which eventually made me smile, I felt more deeply in touch with my love for my father and my vulnerable and more open heart.

I think it helps to manage these sacred openings well: to write about them; to rest afterwards; to spend some quiet time in nature; to share with a trusted friend or family member. But to allow time for recovery and to honour and value the experience of sacred tears is VITAL.

# CHAPTER 19:
# MARCH 2018

ON GRIEVING AND LOSS

I wrote this well over a year ago, right after my Father died. I'm sharing it now, as I know quite a few people who are going through different forms of grief and loss just now. Two pals very recently lost their fathers too - you know who you are. It may or may not be of help to some folks out there wading through the treacle of grief.

And so, the work of conscious grieving begins.

Anticipatory grief, from watching terminally ill family/friends, the slow fading of dementia, or just plain old age creeping in on our loved ones certainly gives us a head start on it. But I know too that there is a deep dig ahead. No-one can protect us from it; no-one can do it for us.

Finding those last texts, seeing old videos/photos, absent-mindedly saying "wait till I tell Dad about that!" rips the freshly formed scabs from the wounds on a daily basis.

There is no doubt that the love, caring, prayers, Reiki and blessings from others surrounds and sustains us. Well, for a while. THEN the journey ahead begins. Alone.

I'm a lucky girl - I have good loving people who have my back. I did plan, and am taking time off now until New Year. Not everyone can do this. How folks with young kids/shift work/ageing parents do this I simply do not know. I will still have responsibilities to deal with. I will call regularly and often, and have to pop in to the clinic now and again. But I know I NEED time now.

There is a darkness ahead that I want to embrace. John of The

Cross talked of "The Dark Night of The Soul."

I'm going to walk a beach at St Andrews tomorrow with my G, sit by a log fire and drink nice wine, eat fish, and sleep in a cosy hotel with warm fluffed-up towels, and plan this precious time.

Already I feel called to the island of Iona for some solitude and to visit the cairn where Dad and I left pebbles last year. G will come for a few days, and then head home. Some things need alone time.

I want to write a letter to my Dad, expressing any unfinished business, hurts, fears, anger, regrets, frustrations, love, joys, memories, gratitude....ALL of it. Then I will read it to the se, and burn it on the beach at the North End.

I want to sit amongst the candles and talk to him, to pray, to cry openly and abundantly.

I want to sleep until I'm spent, walk in the wind and eat Sister Jean's pavlova until I'm stuffed.

I want to walk and hear his voice in the wind.

On my return, I plan to visit his childhood streets, our childhood homes, his special places. I want to photograph some of these places maybe for a calendar. I want to write him a poem, or even a song.

Maybe then I'll be ready to be with my friends who have patiently stepped back to give me the kind of space they know I need.

G and I plan to set off for Lindisfarne (Holy Isle) the week before Christmas to avoid the Spendfest frenzy. Pat, like us, loved it there too in Dark Winter, when the seas cover the causeway and transform it into a magical island again. There is only ONE Christmas tree there. Hurrah!

Then, I hope I can return and hold this Christmas gently, with its welcome return of the light into the world. Maybe I can then, after the new start of the New Year, handle taking up the reins of a busy clinic. The work I love, but can't contemplate at the moment.

I know that a month of conscious griefwork is only the start of the "marathon" of loss of a parent; but it's preparation and training for the long walk ahead. It's finding that rhythm. One breath at a time, one step at a time.

Angela Trainer

God bless you Dad, leave a light on in Heaven for me. I love you. x
Angela Trainer

# CHAPTER 20:
# APRIL 2018

TOP TEN TIPS FOR TRICKY TIMES

1) Cry. It softens and opens the heart. Then, cry even deeper. Make sure you have really cleansed your system and not cut off midstream. Remember nobody has "cried too long" written on their Death Certificate as cause of death; but some may have died as a result of holding it all in.

2) Walk in nature - find a special place that holds and comforts you and just sit there. It expands you.

3) Write down all your feelings, get it all oot – everything! Scroll it then burn. It's very purging.

4) Find some music that expresses how you feel. Sit or lie down and really listen to it. Lose yourself in the music. Sing along and express yourself from deep inside. If you play, do so as therapy - not to perform or entertain - simply as soulful expression.

5) Identify your "Soul Friends" and talk to them about how you feel. These are the people we can say anything too and know it will be held in confidence; that they have no agenda other than our best interests.

6) Create space for some time in silence and solitude. It heals us deeply inside. Look up to the skies - watch clouds, stars - the bigger picture helps to dissolve our dilemmas and heal our broken hearts.

7) Invest in your nutritional needs: fresh, living foods and lots of hydrating water. Vitamin supplements help, especially when we are depleted. Juice and steam veggies, eat some fruit and raw veg as if it were mind-medicine. Because it is!

8) Source some inspiring reading. Charity shops will always have "just the book you need".

9) Establish a good sleep/rest routine. If you can't sleep, sit up and meditate, pray, read your book, listen to some inspirational talks on YouTube… just don't look at the blue light on the screen, it badly affects sleep patterns.

10) Spend some time around animals - they are great healers - even sheep and cows. Birds, bees and butterflies are great intuitive therapists too. Walk near a farm, through woods, visit a zoo or Butterfly World. Cats and dogs are soul-healers extraordinaire - borrow one from a friend if you don't have one.

10a) Know this too shall pass; you are NOT alone. Many others are suffering from exactly the same thing as you, at exactly the same time?

10b) Oh, and find a pal who does Reiki and ask for some. Or find "Harvest Healing Free Distance Reiki" on FB and add your name to the Comments Box. We'll send you some at 10pm each weeknight.

*Feel free to share; someone you know might just need this today.

# CHAPTER 21: MAY 2018

11 May ·2018

THE CONTEMPLATIVE MONK

It's been a deeply meaningful week. There have been so many courageous, trusting people I've had the honour to sit with in a therapy room. And outside of work, others who are soul-friends are going through the grieving process too. For some, their loved ones passed years ago - but the loss is fresh and rekindled by anniversary. Others are still in the cocoon of shock of a recent death. Some are side-blinded and shattered by a sudden, stinging blow of grief which caught them unaware, "just as I thought I was getting over it".

It finally dawned on me: we always are. We are almost always getting over a loss, the end of something, a leaving.

It may not be a physical death, but ALWAYS there is, or has recently been, something ending.

And there may be a pause, just like in-between breaths. Then something is incubating and then something beginning. I read a beautiful article on grief recently.

It said: "it never leaves us; it never disappears and goes away. No, that's not what happens - it's that we grow as a result and therefore it takes up less space of the whole of us, in our expansion. I think it softens us- if we allow that to happen. It expands our heart.

"To hold our pain and our gratitude in the same moment is to draw water out of the deep well of wisdom and compassion."

The Contemplative Monk

So, if you are not actively in a state of loss or grieving at the moment, know that around you many will be. They won't always show it or tell you of their pain. They will find a psychotherapist, like me, and sing their raw heartsongs out in confidence and in private.

But you can help, with a little awareness and compassion: reach out to the people in the hurting places and remind them they are not alone.

"For love to be true, it has to hurt." Mother Teresa

# CHAPTER 22: NOVEMBER 2018

SECOND ANNIVERSARY

ON KEEPING VIGIL

So as the second anniversary of my Father's death nears on Sunday, we are heading to Pitlochry for a couple of days. We went there with him often.

He loved it in the mountains and forests around the historical spa town beside Schiehallion - the ancient sacred site known as "The Fairy Mountain" - interestingly, made of rose and clear quartz crystals.

There I will 'keep vigil' with him.

I wanted to check on the official meaning of the word "vigil" so I did a Google search.

Now, my Dad's name is Patrick. Imagine my shock/surprise/delight when I searched and found this description.

"If someone keeps a vigil or keeps vigil somewhere, they remain there quietly for a period of time, especially at night, for example because they are praying or are making a political protest eg: She kept a vigil at Patrick's bedside."

I've been writing and reading around grief, death and dying a lot as I write my book and today came across author Elizabeth Lesser of The Omega Institute in New York.

She offers some useful practices to help us integrate the little deaths and losses into our lives which help us to build the emotional and spiritual muscle to deal with the actual ones.

She suggests

•Become an 'I don't know it all'.

Whenever you find yourself getting anxious about the big and small deaths of daily life — being out of control, not getting what you want, endings and partings — take a few minutes to allow in the possibility that you do not see the full picture. Often what looks terrible today will, in retrospect, have been a blessing. You do not have to understand or figure everything out. Relax into the mystery of not knowing.

•Disengage from the ego.
Develop a simple meditation practice. Every day, spend some time sitting in silence… Sit with a straight back and relaxed body. Feel the nobility, patience, and strength -Just observe everything.

•Take birth and death back from the experts.
Become familiar with the two bookends of life: birth and death. If you can, be at the births and deaths of family members and friends; sit with sick people; help others who are suffering. Do not shy away from what makes you uncomfortable. Learn about death.

I can testify to the benefits of all three: I doubt I'd have survived thus far without them.
And now, as I head for Schiehallion and Pitlochry I can say I really am away with the Fairies.

ON THE COST OF LIVING AND LOVING:
I know many for whom November and December (the run-up to Christmas) is a difficult time, when a loved one has been lost in this season. I used to say that in my job as a psychotherapist, I could've stayed open and have a queue EVERY day at Christmas/ New Year, with clients who suffer from loss and bereavement issues around that time.
I now personally understand even more fully how challenging these "Festive Family Times" are since my own Father's death two years ago this weekend and the pressures they put many under, who are going through the grief process - at whatever stage: some live and current, some anniversarial, some anticipatory grief (ie

terminally ill).

While Noddy Holder is practising his scales and the bells are beginning to jingle, talk of Christmas shopping and nights out can be triggers that awaken memories and thoughts of who WON'T be there.

Our old friends grief, loss, death and dying give us a shoulder tap and remind us they are around.

I have found Richard Rohr's writing very comforting on the subject of death and dying, deeply healing balm for my soul.

He quotes Thich Nhat Hanh's words, "Enlightenment for a wave is the moment the wave realises that it is water. At that moment, all fear of death disappears".

And also Stephen Levine's: "But water is water, no matter what its shape or form. The solidity of ice imagines itself to be its edges and density. Melting, it remembers; evaporating, it ascends.".

Rohr expands: "So do not be afraid. Death to false self and the end of human life is simply a return to our Ground of Being, to Love. Life doesn't truly end; it simply changes form and continues evolving into ever new shapes and beauty."

To those who are grieving just now out there (you know who you are), remember that you never walk alone and Love NEVER dies.

ON THE EXHAUSTION OF POSITIVITY

We often overdo and definitely over-rate it. We are BOMBARDED on a daily basis on Facebook with ways to do more of it, accompanied by all the happy smiling faces of the picture-perfect people hugging other picture-perfect people, with lockjaw smiles and laughter dimples to die for.

And yes, before you say it, I've posted a few of them myself.

However as a therapist, the New-Age obsession with all things laughter-light-sparkle has kept me in a job for over three decades. How so, I hear you ask, dear reader?

When we suppress and repress so-called "negative" feelings and emotions eg fear, anger, sadness, depression, bitterness, rejection, rage, jealousy.. guess where they go?

The Angels and the Unicorns DON'T actually carry them away to

Planet Sequin for recycling: they go deep into our tissue, our marrow, our psyche, and they rot there, acting like invisible battery acid corroding our core self.

They usually require far more valiant attempts at anaesthetising via the usual methods - alchohol/sugar/drugs/chemicals/spending/punishing exercise regimes/ocd behaviours/obsession with glamour and image/co-dependent controlling systems/even more self-righteous anger, and lots more to keep them in check.

It's that, or we undertake military policing at great cost, of the walls and borders of our denial. This too comes at quite a price. We find emotions leak and haemorrhage embarrassingly at the most inappropriate and awkward times.

Now I feel like the Victor Meldrew of the Alternative Scene.

Positivity is important and it has its place; smiling and laughter, love and lightness of spirit are of tremendous value. But we repress and deny our 'negative' emotions and feelings at our peril. And anyway they can be the illusory masks of co-dependency. "Nice person's disease", as I call it.

We SHAME ourselves for having them (an old childhood trick we picked up way back when) and we BLAME others for having them instead -projection. Thanks Sigmund.

Being unwell and forced to slow down, or even lie down, is a fantastic way of playing catch-up with whatever you've been avoiding deep down.

I re-discovered this one myself this week. Wow- there were some interesting corkers in there trying to find sanctuary and take root!

Self-loathing is not the medicine. Loving, gentle recognition of our human nature is all that is required.

I'm messy. You are messy. And messy is not just a good footballer: it's part of the deal here.

So I'm gonna rewrite a post I found today and celebrate the brokenness; the woundedness and the okayness of all of us in our damaged wee selves.

Here's to the power of messiness. May we risk honest exploration and find the wellspring of power and of passion that may have been dampened and squashed deep down inside, by our Ego's relentless search for perfection and pure positivity.

"Sit on the couch, lie on the bed, crouch on the cushions,
And wait.
Stay in for a while. Don't change a thing.
Release that false grin; drop the adrenalin fixes
Stop doing stuff.
Forget the de-cluttering project.
Accept your own negativity - and in so doing the brokenness of others.
Everyone is trying their best - no matter the distressing disguise they are wearing.
Sit up and watch the light change; the fullness of the moon and mystery of the stars. Just be held there in your messiness.
Have a long lie or a duvet day - but make it luxurious: wear the good jammies; have candles lit as you shower bathe. Soothe yourself with comfort music and comfortmax food.
Embrace your vulnerability- your soft and at times scared wee self.
Have a moan, apologise in advance for bitching - you're raw.
Remind yourself it's okay to be overtired and whiny sometimes - you have an inner child that has needs too.
Be a bit selfish for a while. Avoid anything that looks like a challenge.
Oh, and avoid 'positive' people like the plague until you resurface and decompress.
-Angela Trainer Nov 2018

# CHAPTER 23: DECEMBER 2018

ON NUDGES FROM HEAVEN

So there I am, on the phone to my friend Lorraine, who's been a wee bit lurgied up for a while and we are discussing her full recovery, when I draw up behind this car emblazoned with the words FEEL GOOD at the lights, during the call.

Her business is called Feel Good Factor but the van is nothing to do with her company.

These little happenings are all around us at every moment; but I need to stop and pause, to breathe, to take the time to really SEE the Heavenly nudges; the whispers of grace from the invisible realm that infuses and surrounds me with its web of Love.

Gratitude is one of the highest-ranked resonating emotions for health and empowerment. It strengthens us. It fills us up and raises us up from the minutiae of our 'troubled' lives. It affords us a perspective charged with resilience.

However, making the adjustment from chilled-out-time-off and going through the decompression chamber back to full on work-life is always a challenge for me, at this time of year especially.

I'm a layabout at heart. It's been easy to feel irritated by traffic, deadlines, having to share the planet with other people and increase my speed in dressing/eating/showering, after two weeks of taking half a day to do any combination of said tasks.

I felt righteously justified in my petty grumbling about how hard it was being me and being "too old for all of this" (though not too sure what all of "THIS" actually specifically referred to).

Until I read about someone I know, a friend of a friend, who I've not heard of for a while, who underwent a double hand transplant this week.

Corrine was on camera, tearfully expressing her joy at having her arm stumps transformed by two transplanted hands.

Through her grateful tears she declared her joy at having "fingers she could feel moving".

She is a single mum and quadruple amputee having survived pneumonia and sepsis many years ago.

And she has climbed Ben Nevis and Kilimanjaro amongst superhuman feats and set up her charity raising £700,000 so far for the benefit of OTHER amputees.

Anthony De Mello tells the story of the happiest man he ever did meet: a rickshaw-puller in Calcutta, who beamed a love of life every day as they chatted.

The average life expectancy of said occupation is early 30s. He had just sold his skeleton for money after his death to provide for his family after his demise.

He was soooo happy he could do this for them. His definition of success and joy was if he woke up in the morning, his eyes opened and he was still breathing.

THAT was a wonderful sign. He had been given another day. A gift! Kinda puts it all in perspective, eh?

Take the time to slow-it-down.

In fact just

• STOP.

• Make a hot drink and drink it slowly.

• Acknowledge the shoulder taps in your life.

• Wiggle your beautiful fingers and kiss every damn one of them. Bless them. Thank them. Caress them.

• Say a wee prayer or send a wee invisible blessing to the ones who are REALLY struggling just now (not bemoaning the overfull laundry basket, like me).

• And thank God/The Divine Intelligence/The Universe/Love/The Mystery* for them, your magical and magnificent fingers and the beautiful, inspiring and struggling souls in your circle and beyond.
(* Circle as appropriate )

• Enjoy the afterglow of blessing & gratitude.

THE INVISIBLE WHISPERS OF GRACE
So, it is Winter Solstice: the longest night and shortest day. We decided to go into town.
As we left the subway a fantastic musician was busking and we stopped. He was singing Stand By Me.
This was my Father's favourite film of all time and he loved the song. G remarked on the coincidence and it felt like a shoulder tap.
Tap two: we ended up sitting next to Paolo Nutini for lunch, who also famously sings said song.
Strike three: our day ended with the Christmas market funfair and we found ourselves sitting on the horse carousel ride listening to Chris Rea singing Driving Home For Christmas.
G reminded me of the significance.
For his last Xmas gift to me , my dad got tickets for "Carousel - The Musical" at Pitlochry Theatre. He couldn't come, I thought because of his illness, but he explained later that he had felt far too emotional to endure the storyline.
A Father dies, goes to Heaven and is offered one last day to revisit Earth. He visits his daughter who is really struggling, ostracised by the community, and he sings to her "You'll Never Walk Alone". I nearly melted during the performance and I nearly melted again as I remembered. The Father worked on the carousel horse ride. I've not sat on a carousel ride for years but, strike four, one of the few early photos I have of me as a tiddler... yep, its me and Dad on the horse carousel at Butlinsland.
I awoke too  early this morning with an urge to read the lyrics of "Stand by Me". How apt for a Solstice night. I suggest you do the

same.

Bless you Dad x

# CHAPTER 24: CHRISTMAS 2018

A WEE CHRISTMAS STORY.

If I've not said it already, I wish you a happy healthy Christmas.

I think it is true that Christmas can wave a wand and make things softer, more beautiful, if we allow it to. I had a few 'happenings' during the portal of Christmas.

Shoulder tap number one happened as we left to drive down to Helensburgh to make dinner and celebrate with Mum. She hadn't been feeling too great with the lurgy. I was driving, and reminiscing on Christmases past.

All of a sudden, a bloody big black jeep overtook me and pulled in right in front of me. As I gasped, Lord G declared "Look at the registration plate!".

It was "DAD". Now for the cynics it was "W23DAD".

23 is our joint lucky number, has been for decades; W for WATTS - my slave name, so to speak.

It looked at the time like "WEE DAD" in the rain which is how we all referred to him.

Cut to shoulder tap number two; after-dinner gift-giving.

My Mother gave me the most astonishing gift. A painting of The Tree of Life and the Passage of Time.

It is mahoosive and three-dimensional with old watch faces affixed to some of the branches. It positively shimmers and glitters in the light.

My Mum has NO knowledge of the significance of trees for me, or for Dad in his later life.

His favourite tree is in Perth, in the centre of a huge field, all by itself.

He spoke of it often and years ago G photographed it in the snow at 6am to get the perfect shot for his Christmas, framed as a photo-painting.

I have a dedicated Wishing Tree (Celtic Clootie Tree ) in my garden that we use in the retreats and Reiki courses. My Mum wouldn't really know or remember that.

I also use the analogy of the tree in my work a lot, the healing power of the energy of trees and the metaphor of grounding like a tree with roots in Reiki trainings.

It couldn't have been any more appropriate. But she wasn't to know any of that at all. She took a gamble and played a hunch.

She said: "Time will pass and I won't be here either but you can remember me when you look at this. I can see your Father there too in the trunk with his arms outstretched".

Cue the Christmas Kleenex.

ON A TRICKY TIME

Christmas is a tricky time; all that love and peace malarkey we are supposed to be feeling.

I saw a programme about the Hindu religion recently and arrogantly tutted my judgement about the Caste system: Some are high born, others lower caste and never the twain shall meet.

Then I realised I have my own wee Caste system inside of me. Those who meet my standards and approval, those who don't quite meet my lofty standards (which I don't manage myself) who are "Cast out". Exiled!

When I find the extra room in the smelly old stable in my heart for the broken, the damaged, the 'poor', the vulnerable, or as Richard Rohr says, "the nobodies, those can't play our game of success, who cannot reward us in return", I experience a DEEPER LOVE, from where I least expect it.

I begin to see life through the eyes of my soul.

The nativity story that wee Ella Rose starred in last week (Okay then - she only played the Innkeeper!) says it all.

The Wise people (who says they were men?) on a journey of

searching, The Outcast (Shepherds were just that - unwelcome), the Animals, the shitty smelly stable, the abject poverty of it all, the innocence, the vulnerability, the birth of Love, the messages from Nature, the guiding star - the invisible whispers of grace from the Angels.

What an amazing metaphor -A one stop shop of Pure Gift.

Richard Rohr and Caroline Myss, mentors and writers, both independently remind me that to love is to recognize the sacred in everyone - even those I hold in my Inner Dungeons.

Rohr says: "Either we see Love in everything, or we don't see it at all."

We only see a counterfeit copy of Love.

When I fully stretch my heart and empty my dungeons, my heart gradually expands outwards, widening its loving embrace.

Our outcasts, our 'enemies', our prisoners locked in our inner dungeons are sacred. Love created them too.

The ability to respect the outcast, the poor, whether in finances, in health or spirit; the different, the 'enemy', is the ultimate test of the heart.

And that includes respecting the cattle, sheep, birds, trees and oceans. When love grows and expands, we experience more light within. Everything becomes enchanting. Everything belongs.

As Bono and Bob Marley both sang: there is only one love, one world, one truth. It's tricky but not impossible. It means taking risks, moving position, taming the Ego, guarding the tongue and opening our weary, tired, bruised and damaged hearts.

Last word to Richard Rohr "One Love : All we can do is participate."

# CHAPTER 25: HOGMANAY AND THE NEW YEAR

A WEE HOGMANAY STORY

On the way to the Midnight Reflection Service at the Carmelite Convent in Kirkintilloch, G and I were reflecting on 2018 and our hopes for this New Year.

"I forgot to tell you, I had a dream last night," I said. "Well, half-dream, half-waking. My Dad came with a gift for the New Year. He put a glass in my hand and filled it with water".

We both laughed at the implications

"Maybe I need to drink more - nah it was only water! So maybe I need to help my kidneys next year," I mused.

Imagine my surprise when during the meditation and prayer service, we were asked to pause and to select our own individual small pottery bowls, made by Sister Joanne, which were then filled by Sister Marie Helen with blessed water from a jug.

We were invited to bless ourselves; cleanse ourselves and release the old symbolically and/or drink from the cup and invited to keep it.

It was only on leaving G reminded me of the dream I'd told him about before we arrived there. It had eluded me - the significance, the validation.

As we walked outside afterwards, 30 minutes into the New Year, a thunderous honking of wild geese conducted a fly-past only 15 feet above our heads, drowning out the nearby fireworks in their intensity.

The wild geese were constant companions in the last few weeks and just after my Dad passed two years ago.

The stars were aflame in that same sky. Heaven's fireworks were all lit and on show.

A Happy New Year to you, all the ones we can't see, but can surely meet, when we listen to the invisible Whispers of Grace.

A NEW YEAR'S EVE GIFT

Here is an 'Advanced' Reflective Practice for Ye Olde Hogmanay Clear Oot... but not for the faint-hearted.

Some people get awfy bogged down with clearing out drawers and cupboards; emptying bins and throwing out old clothes at this time of year.

This is folly! A complete and utter waste of your valuable holiday minutes and hours, equivalent to trying to put an Elastoplast on a burst artery, if the objective is Energetic Flow.

Yes, your sock collection will be colour co-ordinated and you'll find the corkscrew more easily in the utensil drawer.

But the temporary elation of order and control will only satisfy your OCD and your perfectionist-driven Ego for a day or three.

If you don't clear out some of the clutter in your heart; if you don't consciously release some of the prisoners in your inner dungeons and torture chambers - where you are still punishing them for offences of many moons ago.

If you don't open the windows of your mind to fresh energy and flow, making space for new challenging attitudes; the promise of trying new things; expanding your viewpoints and horizons.

If you don't do these things then all the clear-oots in the world are a waste of space on an energetic level.

• Light a candle, for illumination, for enlightenment.

• Who do you need to pardon; forgive, release, unshackle? Are there parts of YOURSELF locked up in a cell down in the bowels of your inner castle, denied the light of day?

• What wounds and hurts are you still nursing possessively? What do you get out of that? How does playing victim serve you?

• How much payback do you receive from carefully nursing and nurturing resentment and bathing in the waters of self-pity? It can be really addictive, soothing and comforting - can't it?

• Where and with whom do the seeds of forgiveness need to be planted; how can you prepare the ground within your inner land-scape? Don't forget you may need some self-forgiveness too.

• What have you learned from all of the above?

• Rest and digest. Smile a while.

ON QUIETER TIME
The pop group Herman's Hermits used to sing "There's a kinda hush all over the world"
January and February are hush months, even though there is so much activity incubating deep underground and inside of Mother Nature. In fact the success of Spring depends upon this cycle and time of change and rest from external activity.
Our culture has learned to ignore and command the Seasons of na-ture and set expectations and demands so high that we believe we should be on a productivity and activity level which is the same, regardless of season, weather, light-cycle or temperature.
This is daft - don't fall for it.
If you really must "DO SOMETHING" after the communal en-forced crazy-busyness of the Festive Season, do the Bin A Bag For 30 Days challenge to exorcise the restless, edgy feelings that the quiet of winter descends.
You throw out/recycle/give away a bag of any size full of your excess stuff, whether clothes/books/household/old paperwork/junk.
It doesn't matter whether it's a tiny freezer food bag or shopping carrier right up to a big bin bag - just do it EVERY single day for a month.

This can help to alleviate the restless itch we may experience as we begin to change gears and surrender to gravity and the pull of the Natural World.

•Commit to reading an inspirational book a month.

•Commit to long candlelit soaks in the bath slathered in some of those Christmas gifts.

•Commit to the invention of a new soup combination. I discovered beetroot, Heinz Beans, tinned tomatoes and pickled onions combine well, whilst snowed in with an almost bare cupboard last year.

•Commit to sitting soft and quiet for more extended periods, just because you can.

•Rediscover your music collection: take time to sit down and really listen to some of it. Sing along. Feel the vibes. Dance.

• Find a beautiful journal and write poetry or the story of you, or keep a feelings log and rediscover yourself.

•Take time to check on others who've been unwell - lots of post-viral bunnies around who may be feeling low. Slow down and give them your time or help.

• But mostly commit to changing gear and don't force your body into creating illness as a way to put the brakes on you and save you from yourself.

• Love yourself this Winter. Love Winter. She is a very special season with an awful lot to teach us.


ON EASY DOES IT
January has over time become the month of universal self-loathing.
It's always in someone's interest for you to hate yourself and purge/diet/join a gym/buy exercise equipment/join weight clubs and give EVERYTHING UP - by yesterday!

Why not try loving yourself a little bit more instead and watch what happens. Be gentle. Talk nicely to yourself. Slow it down.
Self-hating, self-loathing and negative self-talk create a hateful tug of war inside - then we seek to anaesthetise our pain with all the old behaviours and substances.
What we resist really does persist.
Baby steps. Try it. Give love and encouragement to your inner baby, one tiny step and tumble at a time.

ON PACING
This is no time for throwing ourselves into cycles of manic activity nor utopian plans and striving. This is a time for retreat and quiet, slow and cosy.
Mother Nature is showing us how.
Withdraw, hunker down. Coorie in.
Ponder and contemplate. Read inspiring books. Journal and reflect.
Meditate and sleep.
Let the winds blow away the dust and cobwebs; let the rains wash and clean; let the snow and ice freeze and freshen. Mother Earth is busy underground and within. So should we be.
St. Angela Trainer of Condorrat

"Close your eyes and follow your breath to the still place that leads to the invisible path that leads you home."
~ St. Teresa of Avila

ON NEW YEAR RESOLUTIONS....NOT!
At Hogmanay, time deepens and it can be a sacred space.
"We desperately need to make clearances in our entangled lives to let our souls breathe. We must take care of ourselves," says writer John O'Donoghue.
If you want to set yourself up to fail, choose the darkest, coldest, skint-iest, post-gluttonous, energetically lowest ebb, immune-system-challenged time of year to get enthusiastic and commit to lots of Utopian goals that will have failed by the end of week one. if you're lucky.

Don't be daft!

You are totally out of sync with the cycles of nature - the seasons and life cycles.

New Year with all its promise of resolutions can become one big party for our inner perfectionist to come out and play - followed by one big disappointing hangover of failure.

Here's Brene Brown: "Perfectionism is not the same thing as striving to be your best. Perfectionism is the belief that if we live perfect, look perfect, and act perfect, we can minimize or avoid the pain of blame, judgement and shame. It's a shield. It's a twenty-ton shield that we lug around thinking it will protect us when, in fact, it's the thing that's really preventing us from flight."

HERE'S ME:

This is a time for emptying, reflecting, hibernating, gestating when it all goes on "underground" and inside.

Take some time, some pens and paper. Light a candle and RE-FLECT.

What did I learn last year? What are the life lessons? What did life teach me? What are THE FRUITS I am CARRYING FORWARD into my New Year?

Who and What am I GRATEFUL for? What are the gifts and blessings I wish to give thanks for this Hogmanay?

What precious treasures have I been gifted on my life journey that I carry with me into this new chapter?

What are my talents and how is my SOUL being called to action in my life? How can I express and share my unique, individual GIFTS more fully?

What is my vocation? How may I SERVE LOVE better and deeper? How do I clear and prepare the ground for that growth and blossoming?

Hogmanay is a great big mahoosive punctuation mark. It can be, if we allow it to, the end of a chapter.

We have an opportunity to close this chapter in our Book of Life. To review and edit, to begin a new updated edition after the revisions, based on current research.

ON THE SEARCHING

This is a time of year when so many of us are making resolutions and deciding that what we really need is yet another new job/partner/car/hairdo/ exercise routine or body shape.

Nothing terribly wrong with seeking something more or new; but it's often futile when what we are often really seeking is a sense of CONNECTION.

We crave a sense of AWE. A sense of the SACRED in our lives. And that is an inside job, it will never be sustained by the externals in our lives in any truly satisfying way.

We simply become 'Hungry Ghosts', as named by Dr. Gabor Mate. We are looking for the next increasingly shorter and faster fix, growing a bigger appetite. We thirst in the dry night of the material world with empty and growling bellies and move on to the next thrill or excitement, hoping to be satiated.

When we practise detaching with love from our busy exterior world, from our ego-driven appetites/our need for competition/perfection/the need to win/from our hurting places/the need to be right, we detach from fear. The fear of lack; the fear of not enough.

Surrender is usually a precursor of healing, a necessary step. And there are many ways to surrender: meditation, contemplation, self-hypnosis, mindfulness and reflection are all ways of surrendering and going within.

Maybe on this bright, fresh, sunny January day, you can detach a little from the fear and go inside a little, with a bit of quiet, space and silence.

And we find in there the still small voice of intuition and wisdom. The voice of Love.

And love will always conquer fear.

ON 'A WOMAN'S PLACE'

There are many paths we can choose in life: too many to count. But there is one which all of us find ourselves on at some point in our lives: the Road Less Travelled.

It's a bit of a Rocky Road, with many twists and turns, sheer drops, steep ascents and steeper descents.

At times it's utterly isolated, and at others friends and strangers join us for part of The Way.

It can be, however, a lonesome road and seem at times like a never-ending journey, that slowly strips away our sense of who we think we are, layer by layer.

Until there is no ME left - at least, not one I recognise.

Life will regularly bring us to our knees. And we do well to find our Sanctuary.

I find my Sanctuary in the woods.

In the forest, I find my 'temple'; the ocean is my cathedral. The hills, lochs and mountains are my sacred ground.

When life cracks us open like a grain of wheat and we are spilled out, it serves us well to sink the tiny tap roots of our heart into the rich and fertile ground and wide open spaces of our Mother Nature, the wildness of wilderness can facilitate the necessary heart-healing we need.

The state of wonder and awe I experience in nature empties me.

I feel very small. Yet I am part of all of it - connected and held.

Perspective changes all by itself. The mind of the small me is re-calibrated and retuned as I let go.

When we 'empty ourselves', we are humbled in the face of Love. And humility is a magnificent state of Grace when we touch it or recognise it in another.

Most of the great inspirational teachers undertook "Descent" - "took the lower place, not the higher place".

They knew their place.

Me? I am still on the road, finding my place, a little more each day.

"Are my boots old? Is my coat torn? Am I no longer young and still not half-perfect?

Let me keep my mind on what matters, which is my work,

Which is mostly standing still and learning to be astonished..."

by Poet Mary Oliver who died this week; though Love NEVER Dies.

# CHAPTER 26:
# JANUARY 2019

We are creatures of habit and we develop pathways in our brain that means we do things in the same rote fashion: eg we tend to brush our teeth the same way; men shave a certain way, we go into "auto pilot".

But recent studies have identified that we have neuroplasticity in our brains. Essentially, our brains are like plasticine and will grow and develop with rehearsal, practice and repetition of new behaviours. But it takes TIME.

If you take off your watch and put it on the other wrist it will feel weird. But do it every day and within anywhere from 10-21 days it will feel normal. If you try to switch back to the original wrist THAT will feel weird! So if we commit to doing something for a month, we can establish new neural pathways in our brain and establish a new habit.

Don't sicken yourself by saying "I'm doing this forever." Just commit to a month. Then it will feel much easier.

Skull practice is essential, as well as skill practice. All good sportsmen and women know this.

Borrowing from Hypnotherapy (my subject) we need to practice visualising compelling images to tattoo on our minds our new co-ordinates.

Use The Carrot and The Stick to establish and navigate the new neural path ways.

Create compelling images and storylines in your mind's eye of WHY you want to change a behaviour: visualise and imagine all the disadvantages of the behaviour you want to change.

It can help to also write out a list of them. What do you want to move away FROM? The Stick. Reinforce regularly in your imagination the aversive images of why you DON'T want to do that any more.

Then, create compelling images of what you will gain in time with the change in place. The Carrot.

Again, it will help to write out a list. What do you want to move forward TO?

Imagine the benefits along the way and how good you'll look and feel after that month you've committed to.

Research, planning and preparation are essential to establish new behaviours. Preparation is everything.

Get rid of temptations; ask others for support, advertise what you're doing, get the things you'll need and that will help, sign up for the class/support group/leave the packed fitness bag/training shoes out where you'll have to trip over them to avoid.

And remember, change is ALWAYS challenged. Anticipate how you (or others) may try to sabotage your success. Have a strategy for how to manoeuvre around temptations. But don't make a crisis out of a blip. Relapse can be part of recovery, if we see these events as feedback for the next step.

The curse of perfectionism is that we don't even TRY, because we are so afraid to fail. It can become a form of emotional constipation.

"Whatever you can do or dream you can, begin it. Boldness has genius, power and magic in it" (attributed to Goethe).

And as Nike like to say, "Just DO IT!"

ON PAYING IT BACK

Some of my friends have not been smiling lately; their hearts are breaking with grief, both anniversarial and pre-emptive. One re-feeling the loss as a first anniversary comes down the track like a train, the other waiting for the dreaded phone call. Both states were so familiar to me. I felt their pain, fresh and raw.

What a privilege it was to be able to sit with my pals, hold their hearts for a while and explore what I could offer to try to help ease their pain. It wasn't much but the little I could offer was gratefully and whole-heartedly appreciated.

We all got to feel a close connection from the vulnerable place. We were standing (or sitting) on Holy Ground.

I was able to share from my own journey with grief, what little I had learned, and offer some tiny compass points.

The whole experience this last few weeks and months has felt like a rite of passage. A circle of Life. A return to the beginning.

These are some of the women who were my scaffolding during and after my own father's dying and death two years ago and the aftermath. They helped me refind my smile and replace the fake-it-till-you-make-it smile I wore for so long.

Its an honour to be able to pay-it-back (or forwards): creating a deeper circle of love as we open our hearts and peel back the veils of our vulnerability.

We show ourselves to each other, tears, snotters and all.

I never intended to write a book about this experience, it just happened, but if it helps even one person to deal with their own situation, then I will be thrilled.

Thank you all for the support through the Journey with and without my Captain, and for reading this book. I hope it brings you joy, comfort, relief and the occasional smile.

Remember, love moves in mysterious ways and she often gives us unexpected opportunities to find hidden seams of gold in the broken places. Love Never Dies.


#loveneverdies

Dad and I at my graduation, Glasgow University 1980

Me, my brothers Raymond & Chris & Dad

My beautiful & stylish mother, who so inspires me & the bravest woman I know

Dad & Margaret with our gang : G, David, Tara, Me & Kim (back row) and Nathan, Ella- Rose And Daniel (front )

The Captain & THAT hat!

Chris, Dad, Raymond & Graham larking about ...when we had 4 of those hats!

Aiden & Ella Rose

My soulmate G and I xxx

## Dad and I on Iona

# ANGELA WOULD LIKE TO THANK

I thank my ancestors, the immigrants from over the sea in Ireland, who started again here in Scotland. I love you.

I'm grateful to my hard, hard-working grandparents whose integrity and spiritual values were handed down via my own parents. I love you.

My Mother is a real heroine of mine. I know her story and her courage and strength still blow me away, in her 80s. Thank you Mum for teaching me about dignity, fortitude and eternal love. I love you. Mum you are a complete inspiration to me, especially on my current journey, as I write this

My Graham. You taught me how loveable I really was. You held me up when I couldn't stand, pushed me forward when I was stuck and cheered me across the line. Your support for me is unwavering. You encouraged me in everything I do since the day we met. And you still make me fuzzy warm inside when I see you. Thank you for loving me more than I could've imagined possible. I love you.

To my brothers Raymond and Chris, who meet me in the music: love never dies. I love you both. You two have the best of our Father in you: his sense of humour, his quick brain, his congeniality, his musical talent, love of your children and your beloved football team. He was so proud of you both. We have many more songs in our hearts still to sing. love you.

My Facebook friends have been the reason this book exists: thank you for your endless comments of support, private messages and encouragement.

This book would not exist without the ongoing harassment of

Monica Smith who refused to believe I didn't want to do it. I love you.

Mark McMurtrie - the idea of a way moving it forward to reality and to Audible was yours. Love you too. Your gentle encouragement and patience in the recording studio were immense.

And as for my Editor Mickey McMonagle, my new Soulpal. We both lost a loved one to pancreatic cancer and Mickey was working on Colin's book when I rang. We both said this was a smooth slide downhill. I'm sure Colin and Pat were greasing the wheels for us. There were long hours, many changes, blips, some hassles - but we had mostly a load of fun and deep chats about life and death. Not one cross word - a record for us both. I love you, and Deborah for sharing you for months. I should really put a wee emoji here - I know how much you love them - not!

To all the proof readers but especially Dave Reynolds (volunteered by wife Shirley). An exemplary retired journalist, Dave took our baby and did the final file and polish. We love you Dave.

Huge thanks to Dorothy Osprey, Elizabeth Harley, Claire Ferguson, Isobel McDonald and Dr.Mary Frame . You offered in a heartbeat and it's not an easy read on a deadline. I love you.

And thank you Judith Lalor for helping to get some PR help to spread the message of the book. I love you too.

An extra special thank you to Marion Duffy, colleague at the Harvest and friend. Well over a decade of support, above and beyond. I love you, Marion.

To Kim, David and the gang - the family I inherited at nearly 40: thanks for making me feel I had kids all along.

To Aiden (5), Ella Rose (4), Nathan, Daniel and all the 'kids', my nieces & nephews (especially Ashley who cried through most of my posts). Dad/Grandad/Pat is so proud of you all, as am I.

So finally, thank you to everyone who assisted, suggested, endured and encouraged this project. To all at The Harvest Clinic, Glasgow who keep our nest warm, to good pals who go back a long way - you know who you are.

Proceeds from this book will go to pancreatic cancer research, thank you for helping.

And always remember: Love Never Dies x

Angela Trainer sees clients privately for Psychotherapy, Hypnotherapy and Counselling and run trainings in stress management,
hypnotherapy and reiki, personal development workshops and
retreat days and weekends.
Contact her at:
The Harvest Clinic
201 St. George's Road
Glasgow G3 6JE
www.harvestclinic.co.uk
0141-333-0878
Facebook Page : The Harvest Clinic

Printed in Great Britain
by Amazon